"The perfect book for every human who dreams big and aspires not only to lead great companies but also to lead systemic change for the benefit of future generations. Jerry challenges us to think more expansively about the role leaders can play in creating enterprises where everyone—including those who have ever been Othered—can feel a sense of safety and belonging, to do the best work of their lives."

—Emily Chiu, COO, TBD @ Block Inc.

"*Reunion* is the book I wish all leaders had in hand—especially during times of social unrest. It's the first playbook I've seen for rewiring how we think about authentically engaging and supporting people from different backgrounds."

—Austin Clements, co-founder and managing partner at Slauson & Co.

"Colonna expands his earlier, stellar work on the psychology of effective leadership to the broader social arena, exploring how we use 'Othering' as a faulty driver of selfhood and a measure of success. Ruthlessly honest, heartfelt, and surprisingly practical, it will make you uncomfortable at times, in the best possible way."

—Jerry Ruhl, PhD, depth psychologist and author of
Living Your Unlived Life

"Brave, vulnerable, and beautifully written, *Reunion* goes where few leaders—especially white men—are willing to go: right to the heart of the challenge."

—Patty McCord, author of *Powerful*

"Infused with empathy, hard truths, and hope, *Reunion* is the manual for human leadership we desperately need. A generation-defining call to action, it will shake readers out of a state of complacency and usher them into a transformational journey that hopefully leaves our world better off."

—David Sax, author of *The Future Is Analog*

"*Reunion* provides a pathway for overcoming separation without pointing fingers or shaming. What makes it brilliant is that it confronts Othering by contextualizing our own stories and ancestry."

—Randy Goodman, CEO of Sony Music Nashville

"This important and powerful book will take you to a new understanding of leadership and a leader's responsibility in creating a place of belonging for all."

—Brad Feld, partner at Foundry

"*Reunion* urges us to redefine our notions of success and leadership and place inclusivity at the center of our work. A powerful reminder of the active role we must play in dismantling oppressive systems, it is a departure from performative actions and a step toward real, substantial change."
—Sope Agbelusi, executive coach and founder of MindsetShift

"Jerry takes us beyond the radical self-inquiry of his first book, *Reboot*, to actively look outside ourselves to challenge the systems around us that unnecessarily (and tragically) separate us from each other. *Reunion* shows us what's possible when we take up the mantle of our highest collective calling: systemic belonging."
—Chad Dickerson, executive coach and former CEO of Etsy, Inc.

"Jerry asks us to revisit our past to become more formidable leaders and, most important, better humans. *Reunion* is a thought-provoking ride that will change how you view the world, your place in it, and what it means to truly create a sense of belonging."
—Laurie Segall, author of *Special Characters*

"Colonna tells his story in a way that will make the reader deeply reflect on belonging, safety, and the things that are truly important in life. *Reunion* reminds us that a fundamental part of being an excellent leader in a business, or in your family, is to lead yourself."
—Lieutenant Colonel Amy McGrath, USMC (Ret.) and author of *Honor Bound*

"Colonna delivers a candid, vulnerable invitation to readers to respond to the fierce urgency of radical self-inquiry, empathy, and inspired action to serve as co-conspirators in creating a new ethos of systemic belonging. It is a timely clarion call out (and call *in*) to the willing, as well as those still undecided, to walk shoulder to shoulder, across our differences, to become the collective catalysts for change and healing our nation sorely needs."
—Shawn Dove, managing partner at New Profit Inc. and co-author of *I Too Am America*

"Colonna guides us to a soaring vista where the pain of our past and the possibilities of our present are both easily seen. The breathtaking view will change how we think and lead forever."
—Dolly Chugh, professor at NYU's Stern School of Business and author of *The Person You Mean to Be* and *A More Just Future*

Reunion

Reunion

LEADERSHIP AND THE
LONGING TO BELONG

JERRY COLONNA

FOREWORD BY PARKER J. PALMER

HARPER
BUSINESS

An Imprint of HarperCollinsPublishers

HarperCollins books may be purchased for educational, business, or sales promotional use. For information, please email the Special Markets Department at SPsales@harpercollins.com.

FIRST EDITION

Library of Congress Cataloging-in-Publication Data has been applied for.

ISBN 978-0-06-314213-8

23 24 25 26 27 LBC 5 4 3 2 1

For Ali—we belong together.
And for Marcus.

There lies the longing to know and be known by another fully and humanly, and that beneath that there lies a longing, closer to the heart of the matter still, which is the longing to be at long last where you fully belong.

—FREDERICK BUECHNER, *THE LONGING FOR HOME*

CONTENTS

Many years ago, in a college course on Socrates, a great mentor said something that's been with me ever since: "Asking 'Who am I?' will help you live a life of integrity, but don't stop there. It's equally important to ask '*Whose* am I?'"

Jerry Colonna, another of my great mentors, addressed the Who am I? question in his 2019 book, *Reboot: Leadership and the Art of Growing Up*. The leaders the world needs, he argues, will come only as they learn how to work with their wounds in ways that make it unnecessary to work them out on others.

Now, in *Reunion: Leadership and the Longing to Belong*, Jerry takes on the *Whose* am I? question. Addressing those of us who identify as white, he pushes the question of Belonging far beyond the cozy confines of "my kind of people." *Reunion* demands that we stop "Othering" whole classes of people in an effort to shore up our wounded sense of identity, a wound that can be traced back to the experience of our immigrant ancestors.

Both *Reboot* and *Reunion* focus on the responsibilities of people in leadership, a topic the author is well qualified to explore. In challenging arenas like venture capital, business development, and executive coaching, Jerry is one of the most accomplished people I know. Add to that his degree in English literature, his grasp of depth psychology, and his Buddhist practice, and you have a wise man with the creative edginess that comes from being Brooklyn born and bred.

But that's not what sets *Reunion* apart for me. I find the book powerful because its author does what accomplished people rarely do. He opens his heart and mind to the challenges of a new day, revisits his previous work, finds it lacking, and does the work necessary to extend its reach.

Employing what Buddhists call "beginner's mind," Jerry borrows the eyes of others—some long gone, some still with us—to look anew at himself, his work, and the world. Then he invites us to a reunion with our abandoned selves—selves haunted by the "hungry ghosts" of our once-marginalized ancestors—and with the alien "other" whom we dehumanize in an attempt to protect our racialized privilege and power.

This is a book on the vital role of community in our lives. But unlike a lot of writing on that topic, it does not begin with a romantic vision of life together. Instead, Jerry writes, it begins "with a knee on a neck." He's referring, of course, to the murder of George Floyd by a Minneapolis police officer.

For many white Americans, the nine-minute video of that horrific murder made it more difficult to continue to look away from this country's endemic white supremacy and white racism. In Jerry's case, the wake-up call took a very specific form:

In the years since *Reboot* was published, it's become clear that, however valid and true might have been my call for leaders to be better humans, it isn't enough to overcome systemic Othering and answer the longing for Belonging.

Part I of *Reunion* asks those of us who identify as white to revisit our ancestors and realize how many of them were branded as lesser beings once they arrived in the United States. Starting with names that got changed on Ellis Island, they became racialized as white, gaining the safety that comes with being part of the dominant class but losing touch with their roots. In the process they also lost their compassion for others who could never "become white" as did Italian, Irish, German, Jewish, and other immigrants. In a word, their identities were "*dis*membered," a condition we carry to this day, a condition that renders us unable to acknowledge our brokenness and our need for one another.

Part II is about "re-membering" the dismembered parts of ourselves. *Reunion* demands that we put ourselves back together by recalling our ancestors, refeeling their fears and hopes, and restoring their and our wholeness by retelling the story of which we are the latest chapter. Do this well, and we lay the ground for a new, more generative encounter with "the other," rooted in the radical notion that across all lines of difference, "your story is my story, too."

Those simple words mark the doorway into active empathy that could help bend the moral arc of history toward Martin Luther King Jr.'s vision of the beloved community. Can that vision be implemented in ways that move it from the realm of pious hope into the world of practical possibility?

Leaders in every sector of our common life—religion, education, business, government—have an opportunity to do exactly that. They have the power to create spaces within even the most oppressive systems where the better angels of our nature have a chance to show up. As they do, we can come together on critical missions where joining hands is not only a means to an end but an end in itself, missions that are defeated by all forms of "Othering."

The gravitational force that can bring us together is, Jerry writes, a "transgenerational longing to belong." As we honor the "hungry ghosts" of our ancestors and invite them to co-create the future with us, we will begin to see harbingers of the beloved community. This is the work of love, truth, and justice in our time, and this book offers a portal into it.

—*Parker J. Palmer*

Cultivating Wildflowers

This book began with a knee on a neck.

Knees have been on necks, of course, since the birth of the nation; we have always kept the Other in "their place." But this knee, this neck, this murder—the murder of George Floyd—seemed different.

It was May 2020, and the world was still processing the shock of the onset of the COVID pandemic, a time when those in power allowed the fear of a virus to metastasize into a crisis of division. Health measures such as face masks and lockdowns morphed into badges of tribalism and separation. And rather than confronting the pandemic and using the crisis to unify, our leaders—people we trust to keep us safe—drove us further apart, undermining an already tenuous sense of Belonging for so many.

The pandemic didn't create the injustice, inequality, or racial and xenophobic divisions that undermine Belonging, but, for some, it made such Othering inescapable and undeniable. (Note: When referring to the felt sense of inclusion—especially within a dominant culture, *Belonging* is capitalized. When referring to an individual's sense of belonging, it's lowercased. I've applied a similar logic to the notion of Othering.")

Othering, a term I first came across when reading the work of john a. powell, the Black scholar who leads the Othering & Belonging Institute at the University of California at Berkeley, refers to the pushing to the margins those who don't fit a community's narrative of what is normal, those identified as *other* than the dominant class.

While I knew this, it took the grainy, shaky, cell-phone video of the murder of George Floyd by a Minneapolis policeman to wake me up to the everyday reality of the systemic Othering that my friends, my family members, and my neighbors experience.

Despite the COVID risks, many took to the streets to protest. Behind my privileged locked gates and the whiteness of my life, I watched as millions of people across the world gathered to demand an end to systemic racism and Othering. I watched, but worried more about the spread of COVID and less about the oppression that forced people into the streets.

And then, one night, my then twenty-eight-year-old daughter, Emma, joined thousands on the plaza outside Brooklyn's Barclays Center. Yelling, chanting, the crowd moved up Flatbush Avenue, intending to cross the bridge into Manhattan and over to the headquarters of the New York City Police Department.

As thousands of protestors marched up the avenue and onto the bridge, riot gear–equipped police on horseback followed. In the middle of the crossing, the crowd started to be pushed back toward Brooklyn by a second phalanx of police coming from the Manhattan side. Emma and the other protestors were trapped.

"Daddy," she texted me. "I don't know what to do. They are coming at us from both sides of the bridge." Thousands of miles away, in Colorado, on the farm I call home, I texted my daughter advice on what to do if she were pepper-sprayed and the contact information for my brother, her uncle, who is a lawyer.

It took a threat hitting this close to home before I fully woke to the reality of the lack of Belonging in our communities. For far too long, I had enjoyed the ability to tsk-tsk my way through the discomfort and pain of systemic racism and the oppressive Othering of those whose bodies, loves, and beliefs did not fit the heteronormative narrative that so dominates our culture. I had been able to turn away from the hegemony of that narrative and its rootedness in, and complicity with, white supremacy and patriarchy.

As I frantically refreshed my text messages, I recalled the exhortation Emma had repeated over the years. Whenever I'd speak of some liberal, progressive stance I was taking—helping entrepreneurs who identify as women, for example—she'd cock her head to the side, give me that fierce look that only a daughter who is onto her father can give, and say, "Dad . . . it's not enough to be an ally. You've got to be a co-conspirator."

That challenge came back to me time and again in 2020. It struck me hard, frankly, as my first book, *Reboot*, found its audience.

In the years since *Reboot* was published, it's become clear that, however valid and true might have been my call for leaders to be better humans, it wasn't enough to overcome systemic Othering and answer the longing for Belonging.

While necessary, it's not enough for us to do the inner work of unpacking our childhood wounds and, with fierce radical self-inquiry, free ourselves from the need to reenact the old stories of our pasts. Radical self-inquiry that stops at the question of how we have been complicit in creating the conditions we say we don't want—a core tenet of my coaching and my book *Reboot*—is insufficient if it fails to look out to the world as it exists and ask how it could be better.

I came to realize that any attempt to answer that first question without applying the same radical inquiry to the world at large—the world as it is—would fail. We must also speak to the longing to belong that marks our organizations and broader society. If not, we will fail to be the leaders the world needs.

Yes, the necessary first step is to see oneself clearly. To use radical self-inquiry to understand why we do what we do. The vital second step is to ask how those of us who hold power benefit from systemic Othering.

Earlier this year, my company compiled research from more than three hundred performance reviews of coaching clients we'd completed across the previous six years. The results are compelling. The dominant area of weakness among all leaders, the area consistently in most need of work, the one area most likely to cause a leader to lose their job and/ or a company to fail, is a persistent lack of empathy. In other words, the most likely cause of failure is the inability to create systemic Belonging within the organization.

But we know this, right? We've all been led by those who simply do not get us. We've all dealt with the consequences of a world in which the civil and human rights of those not like us are routinely, heartlessly stripped away or denied.

But as much as we might even take to the streets to protest these forms of Othering, have we done the hard work of considering our role in the manifest lack of empathy and compassion? Have we looked at the ways in which we have failed to confront the Othering so prevalent in our organizations, our societies, or our communities? More still, have we looked unflinchingly at how such oppression benefits us?

Over the last two decades, I have been focused on the question of how we have been complicit in creating the conditions in our lives we say we don't want. In *Reboot*, further, I tried to lead by showing my own path to a greater consciousness of my complicity in my own struggles, telling stories of others who, in their efforts to become better leaders, did the work of being better humans, of growing into the adults they were born to be.

Building on the personal work I did with my then psychoanalyst, Dr. Avivah Sayres, I explored questions such as What am I not saying that I need to say?, What am I saying that's not being heard?, and What's being said that I'm not hearing? Later, as an executive coach, I applied those questions to my work with organizations and asked clients to consider how such questions showed up in their lives.

Such questions, as well as seeking to understand the role our unconscious plays in directing our lives, were and still are rare in the literature that defines leadership.

But rarer still are the questions designed to see the ways that our untended wounds, our internalized lack of Belonging, exacerbate the Othering of those not like us.

This must change. It is time we recognize how our traditional definitions of leadership maintain systemic oppression and Othering. It's time for a new definition of leadership in which inclusivity and equity are at the center of our actions as leaders so that Belonging may flourish.

Why do we gather ourselves into businesses and organizations? Root down into the core motives, and we often discover a need to keep ourselves safe by piling up wealth. There are other motivations, of course; we build for the joy and beauty of creation, to manifest dreams, for a greater sense of community. But the root wish for many is to satisfy the human need for safety above all. Indeed, so primal is the wish for safety that we'll fixate on our physical needs, often believing that financial safety is the way to meet our bodily needs. Money becomes a symbol of safety. Unfortunately, our wish for safety is deeper than physical well-being. It is existential. We long to feel safe at our very essence, the longing to belong is bone deep. It is only by knowing to whom and where we belong that the longing is answered.

But what if we expanded the purpose of our efforts beyond self-preservation and our existential safety? What if we dedicated ourselves to creating equitable Belonging? After all, the longing to belong is essential to each of us, and, unfortunately, it is too often denied.

Be warned, though. Expanding our definition and consciousness of the responsibility of leadership in this way will cause a reckoning with the accepted notions of success: output, outcomes, and return on investments. Doing so will necessitate a new definition of success in which inclusivity is central.

In *Reunion*, then, I'm calling for nothing less than a transformation of the traditional definitions of leadership. It's no longer sufficient to measure success by financial return on investment.

A good leader, I contend, uses the experience of leading others, of wielding the privilege that comes with power, to confront their own demons, which could otherwise create toxicity for those they lead. But a great leader actively confronts Othering wherever it sprouts, including from their own inner demons.

THE WAY TO REUNION

The word *reunion* is a noun. But as I am using it, reunion is also a process. Undertaken well, this type of reunion supports the lifelong leadership practice of fostering systemic Belonging. The process of this reunion consists of:

- Using the tools of radical self-inquiry that I describe in *Reboot* to understand the truth of your ancestors' experiences as well as how that truth reverberates in *your* life and leadership.
- Curiously exploring one's past to know the truth of your origins.
- Re-membering the dismembered parts of ourselves, taking back that which was placed into our psychological shadows so that we may show up whole and authentic as well as trustworthy and open.
- Defining leadership as *for* the Other by understanding the true costs of systemic Othering and listening for the longing to belong that is in our organizations and societies.
- Leading, frankly, as a coach might when asking questions and listening deeply, intuitively, and somatically, in our bodies, all the while resisting the impulse to fix the conditions that make so many of our organizations psychologically unsafe.

When a leader fixes people, situations, and organizations, they may inadvertently turn people into problems, fostering an unhealthy dependency on the leader while avoiding a true and lasting transformation. Just as we ought not to "fix" people, but rather enable them to grow themselves, a leader's job is to create the conditions for the organization to undergo the same growth, the same development.

In undertaking this process, we must be willing to be wrong in our assertions and, when that becomes clear, respond with curiosity and a lack of defensiveness. What's more, we who hold power must also be willing to go first, to share our stories so that we may create the conditions needed so others may be able to share their stories. When we do, we create safety—without which there can be no love, no Belonging.

To show how this works, I've organized *Reunion* into two parts. Part I explores our ancestors. It begins by looking at the folks who came before us, who still show up through the gauze of myths and the fables told around holiday tables.

Such myths and fables often involve an idealized version of the old country. "Back there," we tell ourselves. "That's where we belonged." Back there, before whatever it was that sent our ancestors here, we knew Belonging.

Indeed, such myths of the resilience of our ancestors—lacking any recognition of the privilege that may have made their assimilation easier—separates our ancestors from those who were Othered. Such myths then merge into a toxic and sometimes murderous blend of patriotic exceptionalism. For a powerful retort to fabled better times implicit in the phrase "Make America Great Again," consider Langston Hughes's poem, "Let America Be America Again."

O, let America be America again—
The land that never has been yet—
And yet must be—the land where every man is free.
. . .
O, yes,
I say it plain,
America never was America to me

The reunion process requires that you clearly see that, for so many, America was never America. Look around you; for far too many of your colleagues and employees, America never has, and is unlikely ever to be, America for them. Acknowledging this destroys the myths of exceptionalism and sameness while tilting at the structures of disunion and separation. I learned this as a boy.

When I was in high school, a group of mostly white friends participated in a weekly peer group exploring racial divisions at our school. The outside facilitator, a Black man, met weekly with twelve of us.

I'll not forget the moment when, parroting what seemed the right thing to say, I spoke of how we were all the same, under our skin. I parroted what I had been taught, even though in my heart I knew it wasn't true.

"That's a myth," the facilitator said, startling me. "While our lives may be similar, we are not the same." While we may want the same things, he noted, we are not the same. And honoring difference, like recognizing the truth of each of our experiences, doesn't drive us apart but brings us closer together. It reunites us.

Reuniting with that truth, another step in the process, must therefore include encountering our true origin stories—the truths that our ancestor myths shroud and protect us from.

It's not enough to be aware of the truth of our past or the facts of our lives and of those of our ancestors. We must experience the consequences of that knowledge so that we may rise from the unconscious-laden mythmaking and ancestral fables and consciously direct our lives. For years, through our wisdom traditions, our elders have guided us to do this work. Too often, though, we have failed to listen.

"In the church I come from, which is not at all the same church to which white Americans belong," wrote James Baldwin in his essay "The Price of the Ticket," "we were counselled, from time to time, to do our first works over."

To do our "first works over," he says, is to reexamine everything. "Go back to where you started, or as far back as you can, examine all of it, travel your road again," he continues. Tell the truth of your journey, and that of your ancestors. "Sing or shout or testify or keep it to yourself: but *know whence you came*."

This, he noted, is what most white Americans won't do. For far too many, doing this work—examining the truth of our European ancestors' movement from Othered to Othering—risks our tenuous hold on our own Belonging. Regardless of the risk, this is what those of us who hold power—those of us whose ancestors passed through the ambiguity of nonwhiteness, non-American, immigrant status into the privileged safety of Belonging to whiteness—must do.

Embarking on the reunion process means being willing to do such first works over.

This work demands that we understand the stories of those who may have abandoned us as well those who claimed us. So much of the behavior that fosters systemic Othering, so much of what is toxic about leadership, for example, stems from having been abandoned, unclaimed, or left bereft by true elders. When parents, grandparents, and others who could have steered us away from wrong and toward right are gone, what's left are what Buddhists would call hungry ghosts, wraithlike empty shells of adults. Lost and unremembered elders leaving behind hungry ghosts with power. Hungry ghosts wreak toxic havoc on people and their lands.

The toxicity necessary for systemic Othering manifests in several ways. As noted, there's the lack of empathy. But there may also be a refusal to advocate for those who have less power. Fearing a loss of "what's mine," we look away when those who have less, suffer. Those whose Belonging seems tenuous may also manipulate the entire organization into a mechanism to assuage their needs.

Part I ends with an exploration of our dismembered selves, the banished parts of ourselves that lie hidden in the denied memories. Reunification with oneself fosters the union with the dismembered, disinherited, dispossessed . . . be they Koreans in Japan, the Japanese in the United States, Indigenous folks trying to withstand the ravages of a pandemic, immigrants from Latin America seeking shelter and safety, or the descendants of enslaved people stopped by police for a minor infraction, praying in a church in South Carolina, or shopping in a supermarket in Buffalo, New York.

We are often not who we say—or even think—we are. And the origin stories we grow up with cloud our view of who *they*—our parents, our grandparents, all of our ancestors— were, therefore, to whom we belong. Though it might hurt, taking in more of the truth is in service to overcoming separation and disunity. Throughout the book, I share personal experiences as well as experiences from some of my clients in service of overcoming separation and manifesting the world we'd like to see.

OVERCOMING SEPARATION

For this is our ultimate task: reuniting with those from whom we have been separated and overcoming the disunity that comes from the racialization, classification, and Othering of individuals. We meet this task not to further promulgate the myths of sameness but to provide the basis of a leadership that is of, for, and about the well-being of the dispossessed and disinherited.

Part II of *Reunion* is designed to overcome this separation and provoke an encounter with the other.

I have tried to learn from those who have come before in the struggles against systemic Othering. Writers and teachers such as bell hooks, john a. powell, Parker J. Palmer, Howard Thurman, and many others have challenged me to go beyond what I thought I knew, thought I understood, and hear stories I was socialized to ignore.

But the teachers from whom I have learned the most have been those readers who've reached out to me in the years since *Reboot* was published. There was, for instance, Joy-Tendai Kangere, a barrister whom I met in Dublin. She startled me when, after a book reading, she'd said to me, "Your story is my story."

Joy-Tendai grew up in Zimbabwe and immigrated to Ireland, and I couldn't understand how she could feel such kinship with my story. I couldn't understand how she saw her own story in that of a kid from Brooklyn.

Over time, however, I came to understand the empathetic bridge that can be built when those in power authentically admit their struggles to feel worthy of love, safety, and Belonging. I went first and, in doing so, helped make it safe for her to follow.

Over and over again, readers wrote to me saying, in one way or another, "Your story is my story." Over time, that phrase became an affirmation of the interconnectedness, the interdependency of all beings, our inter-beingness.

The work of the only leadership that ultimately matters brings us into this state of persistent, universal interdependent inclusiveness where our stories reunite us.

I owe it to these folks to be silent no more. As so many have taught across the decades, whether it's about the epidemic of AIDS or the horrors of the Holocaust, silence from those who hold power serves the oppressor.

"Evil comes from a failure to think," wrote Hannah Arendt in *Eichmann in Jerusalem: A Report on the Banality of Evil*. "It defies thought for as soon as thought tries to engage itself with evil and examine the premises and principles from which it originates, it is frustrated because it finds nothing there. That is the banality of evil."

A failure to think as well as a failure to feel and then to act. And in such failure we end up cooperating with evil, joining, as Martin Luther King Jr. noted in his essay "The World House," the "protectors of the status quo" and the "fraternities of the indifferent."

In the fall of 2022, the Edelman Trust Institute, in collaboration with Harvard Business School's Institute for the Study of Business in Global Society, documented a profound shift in the expectations employees have of their leaders. Their findings mirror the experiences of my clients, most of whom are CEOs.

As protests against racial inequity, systemic racism, and

the denial of civil and human rights have grown, so have the calls for business leaders to *do something*; the expectations of our colleagues and our employees have changed. More than 70 percent of people surveyed said that businesses should be organized for the benefit of all stakeholders and not just to maximize financial returns.

More telling, though, is the expectation that to be a leader now means one must speak out. More than 70 percent said that CEOs must contribute to the debates and that they need to lead in creating social change, especially on issues such as systemic racism and oppression. Your Slack channels are buzzing with angry employees who are disappointed and expect you, as the leader, to condemn the banal evil of disunion, disinheritance, and separation.

Silence from the well-meaning, well-intentioned members of the dominant classes is no longer acceptable. We must speak up. We must take sides. As Elie Wiesel wrote: "Neutrality helps the oppressor."

More than with *Reboot*, *Reunion* is my attempt to do my first works over. It is my way to speak out and encourage you to do the same.

I wrote in the introduction that reading *Reboot* "should feel like a coaching session . . . a time to step away from habitual and long-held patterns, using tools of inquiry that tap into your unconscious mind, unmask you, and that can enhance your sense of community, which is essential to healing."

In contrast, I hope *Reunion* is like a workshop. The aim of this book is to build upon honest self-reflection and move beyond being a better human, and to heed the call of my daughter, Emma, and her peers to be co-conspirators for systemic Belonging.

As with any workshop, the process requires audience participation. Workshops work because they create emotional experiences, necessary components for any transformation. Cognitive awareness of the need to confront systemic Othering, with carefully constructed arguments, is vital. But it is only a first step. If it is not followed by a felt sense of the need for change—in this case, the tangible, emotional, financial costs of disunion—then change becomes a labor of forced intellect. It becomes performative.

WILDFLOWERS

It was the last night of boot camp, and the group that had come together so beautifully, so openly, were sitting around a fire. As can happen at these camps, these immersive leadership development retreats, guitars appeared like magic out of the dark night. First one, then another boot camper started gently strumming.

Soon enough, we began singing Tom Petty's "Wildflowers": "You belong among the wildflowers," we sang, ending with "You belong somewhere you feel free."

Our companies and our communities should be fields of wildflowers where heterogeneity and the myths of exceptionalism, supremacy, and sameness are all tossed aside for the glory of interdependent, interconnected difference.

We who strive to lead cannot heal all that ails the world, but we can heal more than we pretend. We are not as helpless as we've convinced ourselves. When companies embody the notion that otherness is not a threat but an opportunity, when the sacred promise of work is manifested in the ability of broken-open-hearted warriors doing the work of their lives, then all those with whom we spend our days will be somewhere they feel free.

Being fierce with the reality that lies behind this truth is a cornerstone of better leadership as well as true adulthood. Even wise elderhood.

To do this work is to do the most important task of a lifetime: to put your shoulder to the wheel and move society closer to what is possible. Not to do this work is to condemn the disinherited and inherited alike to division, dismemberment, and needless suffering.

What is the role of a leader if it's not to heal such division? Why do we grow into adulthood if not to make the world better for our descendants? Do we do inner work only to heal ourselves? If we heal only ourselves, what kind of people are we? As Rabbi Abraham Heschel taught, racial prejudice, systemically oppressive Othering, is a denial of God.

Some may say that the divine has no place in the workplace, but I think such complaints are merely expressions of the insidious movement of profit over people, of output over consequence.

Dismemberment, disunion, separation, and Othering are source material for what ails us. Such setting apart leads to the colonizing mindset, the settler attitude, with a relentless pursuit of greater and greater productivity.

Reuniting with our past, our truths, the othered parts of ourselves . . . this is the journey to systemic Belonging. This is reunion.

Having the pulpit of a book, having a body where power is projected onto me because of my gender and whiteness, means I have a responsibility to go first. So I'll go first. In doing so, I hope to shout this call to action for others who also hold power to hear.

Each of us has a responsibility to live up to the true meaning of leadership. The full measure of a leader is more than return on investment, it's a continuation of the expectations built on the anxious and insecure need to constantly prove worth by measuring our lives in what we have colonized, what and who we have dominated, and the toys we've collected at the end of our days. One measure of a true leader is the number of people who feel safe enough to belong.

Tactical, transactional management has a place in our societies and our organizations. We use these skills to build roadways and bridges, to ensure that we have clean drinking water and the vaccines necessary to provide protection from pandemics.

But management that lacks a relationship to the deeper purpose of leadership ultimately fails to effect the changes in society necessary to give each of us the sense that we are loved, that we are safe, and that we belong.

Getting to the hallowed ground of persistent inclusivity is not for the faint of heart or the weak-kneed. Indeed, we may never arrive at this place. But honestly addressing the question of the ways we have been complicit in—and benefited from— the conditions that would allow one group of people to enslave another, to exploit poverty, and to further the otherness of those on the margins is the only path to building the inclusive world our children and grandchildren deserve.

You and I, all of us, have no choice but to do our first works over.

We may falter. We may fail. But, as Robin DiAngelo, writing in *White Fragility*, notes, fear of doing it wrong, of failing to say something correctly, holds back the well intentioned from saying anything at all. Once more, and never forget, silence is evil. Silence encourages the tormentor. Silence equals death.

If I fail in my endeavor, it won't be because I was silent or afraid of being wrong. Let us not fail because we didn't try.

One of the exercises my colleagues and I use at our camps is to send participants out on a walk. We give specific instructions about how to listen. Importantly, and wherever we can, we encourage people to walk side by side, shoulder to shoulder, so that when they share, they are better able to hear their own story in the story of the other. This shoulder-to-shoulder stance heals. It creates in each participant a sense that we are in it—the work that's before us—together.

Let's imagine we're taking a walk together. Let's imagine the cadence of our steps fall into rhythmic rapport so that our bodies, our nervous systems, feel safe.

Come. Let's take a walk. Hear my story of Belonging so that I might hear yours and you might hear your own. And then, together, we can hear the longing to belong in those all around us.

PART I

To Whom Have
We Belonged

CHAPTER 1

The Fig Tree

*May you allow the wild beauty of the invisible world to
gather you, mind you, and embrace you in Belonging.*
—JOHN O'DONOHUE, *FOR BELONGING*

A few years back, on the anniversary of the attacks of 9/11,
a few months after the release of my first book, *Reboot*,
I was headed to an event just north of the 9/11 Memorial &
Museum at Ground Zero when I noticed paper cranes rock-
ing gently in a light breeze, moving like whispering ghosts,
perched on the slabs of black granite that rim the empty space
just above the falling water, the water falling like tears into
the great void. They'd been placed beside the names of people
of Japanese ancestry who'd died in the attacks. As it was on
that day long ago, the weather was crisp and clear—perfect
apple-picking weather. When I saw the paper cranes, my heart
ached, my breath staggered, and I steadied myself against the
edge. Leaning forward, I traced the names carved in the granite. "All these names," I thought, "all these people . . . they're
ghosts."

The weather, the cranes, the negative space of the foot-
print of the old towers, and the ghosts—mostly the ghosts—
transported me back to that morning in 2001. I'd been on

one of the last flights out of New York that morning. I was in Washington, seated at a power table, when word came of the first tower having been struck: "Senator, we have to go," said an aide to my breakfast companion. "The United States is under attack."

After watching the towers fall on TV, I began a twelve-hour trip back to New York, to my family, to my life.

Seeing those paper cranes some eighteen years later tenderized my heart, making it raw and receptive. I stood silently and thought of those who left and of those left behind. One last glance at the cranes and I moved on.

I'd arrived early for the evening's event. It was to be a talk about the ways we can use the journey of leadership to reboot ourselves and reconsider our lives so that we might fully actualize and grow into the adults we were meant to be. Better humans, I asserted, are better leaders, and the journey to leadership should be a journey to full adulthood.

I'd prepared a few talking points, laying out the ways in which our beliefs shape our leadership styles as well as our adult selves. The audience, about a hundred people, had gathered partly to be educated, partly for the wine and cheese.

My talk ended, and my host asked a question about being more productive. Instead of answering, though, I probed the ways his busyness served him. "Why is it so important to be productive?" I asked. I couldn't help but coach him.

This was a familiar back-and-forth. I often resist answering directly when a coaching client asks me to tell them what to do. Instead, I'll turn the question back on them, helping them find their own answers. It's a necessary part of the process.

We then fielded questions from the audience. Each question took the people in the room deeper into introspection and their

own radical self-inquiry; each brought an intimacy that, I suspect, few gingerly holding their wineglasses had signed up for.
Looking at his watch and squirming as the conversation grew
deeper, my host abruptly ended the question-and-answer
period.

Then a movement to my left caught my eye. A woman a few
rows back from the stage had raised her hand multiple times
throughout the Q&A, and my host had, consciously or not,
overlooked her. But I saw her. I pointed to her: "No. We have
one more."

The woman stood, shaking slightly. Her body seemed to
struggle to contain her emotions. What's more, she seemed
determined to speak despite those emotions, despite the
whispery voices in her head telling her, perhaps, to hold her
tongue.

"What I'd like to know is this," she began, her voice stam-
mering a bit. "What I'm struggling with is . . . I mean, I see
my subroutine . . ." she said, referring to my term for the piece
of programming laid down when we are children, the earliest
form of our belief systems that defines how we lead our lives.
Beliefs that our ancestors formed in their efforts to stay safe,
feel loved, and—despite shame, poverty, or forms of Othering they may have experienced—to know that they somehow
belonged.

"I see how my subroutine tells me over and over again I am
not worthy," she continued. "But what I really want to know is
this: How do I stop it?" she asked. "I want to know how I can
feel sufficient, just as I am."

Her words echoed a line from *Reboot*: "How can I know
that, just as I am, I am enough?"

I paused as the room went silent. Wineglasses stopped

tinkling. The chattering stilled. She'd spoken not just for herself but for others.

In the pause, I thought of Ji-Ho, a young woman, an immigrant from Korea, who'd come to one of my boot camps yearning to be a better CEO. A few years before, she'd founded a software company designed to help neurodiverse kids learn math and language skills. Kids like her son. Her self-doubt, her nagging sense of unworthiness, impeded her from taking her seat as the openhearted and brave leader she was born to be.

"I hold myself small," she'd told me on a walk at the boot camp. I felt that self-imposed smallness from the minute we'd met. She seemed too young, for example, to be a CEO. She was thirty-five, though.

"How might holding yourself small have kept you safe?" I asked. When she responded with a puzzled look, I added, "How might holding yourself small have benefited you?"

She paused in midstride and told me of her grandmother in Korea. A woman who'd survived not only the degradations of occupiers from Japan but the dehumanization by the American soldiers stationed there to beat back forces from the northern part of the peninsula—families occupied and dehumanized in service of a global game of power.

Being small kept them hidden. And in being hidden, they were safe. But it also kept them in check; different knees on different necks, perhaps, but still determining who lives and who dies, all the same. Being small, questioning one's worthiness, was a survival strategy.

I knew this subroutine; growing up, I had deployed the same strategy.

For years, my life was marked by the persistent sense that I was nothing—for example, if I wasn't doing *something*, accomplishing *something*—and that the clear sign of my worthiness was what I had accumulated, more than, say, how my family felt. Our stories—Ji-Ho's and mine, as well as that of many of those in the room—mirrored one another.

Earlier in the evening of the book reading I'd explained that as children, to belong to the people who cared about us, we adopt their beliefs. "If we don't maintain the beliefs," I noted, "we run the risk of not only being thrust from the family but, worse, abandoning those with whom we seek connection." Such abandonment feels like a betrayal, for example, of a grandmother who kept a family safe despite two occupying armies or a great-grandmother who guided the family through the Jim Crow era.

One of my subroutines, for example, was the belief that anger is dangerous, and so therefore it was safer to be anxious than to be angry. I learned this by watching my parents' tirades, their outbursts. It took me years to come into a healthy relationship with my necessary and safety-inducing anger.

One of yours, for example, might be that the best way to feel good about yourself is to be in service to others, nearly exclusively, until you diminish yourself into a small, unlovable speck. I call these beliefs subroutines because, like the first lines of code laid out to create a program, they often persist well into multiple generations of the application, only to create a wasteful layer of technical debt; compute cycles are wasted running routines no longer necessary, viable, or true.

Back at the reading, the overlooked woman to my left went on: "I can even see, for example, the way that subroutine makes me accept work for less money than it's worth or, worse, to do things I don't really want to do for little or no compensation."

I paused, took in a breath as well as I considered her frustration at years of being devalued and overlooked, as well as whatever story she told herself about being responsible for her own diminishment. I asked her name. "Lily," she replied.

I felt our connection deepen. Giving someone your name can be like giving them the key to your heart. Receiving someone's name is a responsibility; the intimacy should be held like a treasured bird.

"Lily," I said, using the precious gift of her name, "did your parents carry the same belief about themselves . . . that they weren't worthy?"

"Yes," she said, remembering them. I could almost see her parents' eyes in her eyes, their ghosts merging with her body.

"Did your grandparents?"

"Yes."

"And how about their parents? Did they also carry that belief?"

Lily paused. She stared straight ahead. Then she spoke steadily and from a deep well of frustration and incredulity, as if she were once again being overlooked and unseen. Thinking back on that moment, I see the courage and persistence she must have had to muster to keep raising her hand, again and again, waiting to be called on, waiting to be seen. I can imagine that entire set piece—raising a hand, being overlooked, and waiting to be seen—as something terribly, exasperatingly familiar. She spoke as if what I didn't see was unbelievable, and in that disbelief was a power: "I am descended from Africans who were brought to Haiti as enslaved people. What do *you* think?"

I stopped and took in the righteousness of her incredulity. I may have seen her in the audience, but I had not seen all of her.

Least of all, despite my efforts otherwise, until she'd raised her hand, I wasn't conscious of the bitterness of the intergenerational trauma from hundreds of years of systemic Othering by people who likely had bodies that looked like mine.

"Lily, as a white man, with all the power and privilege that come from that racialized identity," I said, "any attempt to come up with an answer might be bullshit, but because you deserve a response, I'll share what I can, what I see.

"I see your parents, your grandparents, your great-grandparents," I began, "all standing behind you, right now, in this moment."

I asked her to close her eyes to see them with me. "They're standing behind you, not as unsettled ghosts with unresolved pain and suffering, but as resolved, strong ancestors."

Our work of diving into our past, of radically inquiring within, does more than release us from the demands of those subconscious subroutines, allowing us to choose who and what we are to become. It also provides us a chance to turn the ghosts of our past, the ghosts who wrote those haunting subroutines, into ancestors. Ancestors who want us to let go of the very beliefs that kept them safe, made them feel loved, and make us feel like we belong.

"Your ancestors are reaching through time," I told her. "They're placing their hands on your back. They are touching you, their descendant, and they have one wish for you. What's that wish? What would they like for you?"

With her eyes closed, her heart opened to the pain of what her ancestors experienced and her back strengthened by their love, their wishes, their dreams for their descendants, she said, "That I know I am enough, just as I am." She then burst into tears.

As much as we need to feel our ancestors' love for us, we also need to understand who they were and all they experienced.

Understanding who they were makes their love palpable, real. Acceptance of the past—ours, yes, but equally, if not more importantly, that of our ancestors—allows us to feel their hands on our backs.

For years I've asserted the simple truth that better humans make better leaders. As simple as that truth is, though, it's a struggle for us to be better, to grow up and into the fully actualized adults we were born to be. Doing so means we have to face the unfinished, unsorted parts of ourselves that we'd rather ignore. We would much prefer keeping the door of that messy closet shut and would rather not rummage through the trunks of our discarded past, despite knowing that doing so gives us the chance to finally understand why we do what we do.

Now, though, having met folks like the woman who struggled to know that, just as she is, she is enough, and whose ancestors still haunt her, remaining unresolved ghosts, I've come to know that to lead with the integrity the world needs, better humans must also use their power to create love, safety, and Belonging for all those around them. Those three elements—love, safety, and Belonging—are our birthrights, and protecting them is a moral imperative.

One day, a young Black man named Justin wrote to share how much *Reboot* had meant to him. In the conversations that followed he recounted that, in addition to his work as a teacher in a local college, he was deeply involved in diversity, equity, and inclusivity coaching within organizations. We spoke about his work, and, in doing so, he gave me a deeper understanding of the assertions I'd made about our universal needs.

"Inclusivity," Justin helped me see, "is the felt sense of love, safety, and Belonging."

Leadership is more than the culmination of our own growth into adulthood. It is a calling, a demand, to create beloved and inclusive community where all may feel they belong.

YOUR STORY IS MY STORY

Another afternoon, outside a venue in Denver where I was to hold a fireside chat about themes from *Reboot*, I was approached by an older white woman who walked with a cane.

"You look like our speaker," she said while walking up to me.

Laughing, I said, "That's because I *am* your speaker."

She stuck out her hand to shake mine. "Well, my name is Margaret. I grew up in Oklahoma. My parents survived the dust bowl, and I want you to know that your story is my story."

Months later, I was in Dublin for a book reading. The room was filled with folks who'd be identified as white. Those who had hair would be called blond. It was, after all, Ireland.

There was one woman who stood out in that very white space. A Black woman sat in the front row, very close to the stage. At the end of the talk, at the end of the question-and-answer period, she made her way to the front and introduced herself. Her name was Joy-Tendai. She brought the conversation to a point I had discussed, a point about the effect of the loss of an elder at an early age and the tendency for a child, then, to become "parentified," hanging their own sense of Belonging on the perceived well-being and safety of others, especially our elders.

When those whom we are tasked to care for are absent, our sense of our purpose, our meaning, even our Belonging are often shattered. The negative space of absent elders—parents, grandparents, or other sources of wise and safe Belonging, for whatever reason—shapes us all.

"That story," said Joy-Tendai. "That's what happened to me.

"My father died when I was thirteen," she went on. Then, holding my gaze, steadying herself as she reunited not only with her younger self but with her late father, she added, "He was killed on Robben Island." The island prison in South Africa. "Later I immigrated to Ireland from Zimbabwe."

Stunned, I leaned in as she shared the stories of her childhood, of her mother, and of her father. "I wanted you to know because your story is my story."

"Your story is my story," reverberates in me like a mantra. Lily, the brave descendant of enslaved folks, Ji-Ho, Justin, Margaret, and Joy-Tendai—each of these folks resonated with the expressed wishes for the safety of Belonging, of knowing that, just as they are, they are enough. As I encounter more people who experience a similar resonance, I realize that implicit in the assertion that "your story is my story" lies the possibility of a shared experience.

Realizing that possibility, embarking on this process I call reunion, requires using the tools around which I've built my life and my work, the tools of curiosity and radical self-inquiry. The gift of curiously exploring the roots and effects of your subroutines is the knowledge implicit within your own story. Then, from that ground, one might see and feel others' stories. And within that seeing lies the possibility of systemic, inclusive, and persistent Belonging. Your story is my story becomes the bridge to our Belonging to one another. In such reunion is the felt sense that we are not alone. And in that no-longer-aloneness lies the seedbed of a greater, systemic Belonging.

MY ANCESTORS

Living into that possibility, manifesting my part in the seed-bed of loving, beloved community and inclusivity requires that *I* reunite with *my* ancestors, to do the work of turning them from ghosts into ancestors. Then, and only then, can I turn the silent ancestors into whispering and wise elders, all while feeling their hands on *my* back.

For, as is always true with those who seek to help others, I can't ask others to do something that I am unwilling to do myself. My pursuit of helping create a greater Belonging requires that I understand the whole of my story, to reunite with those to whom *I* belong.

To whom do I belong? Well, among others, there's my grandfather, Dominick Guido. One of the ways we can understand to whom we belong is to imagine their lives. To use empathy and our active imagination to step into their experience. If your ancestor crossed an ocean to land in the United States, escaping oppression or poverty, can you step into their experience? Can you use your imagination to feel their story? By turning to those who have come before us, by imagining their story of crossing the Rio Grande, for example, their stories of pursuing love, safety, and Belonging can become the basis of *our* Belonging.

So take a walk with me as I imagine my way into the story of my ancestor. And as is true with so many of the stories of my life, this one begins with a tree.

Dominick cradles the cutting from the fig tree as the steamer from Naples navigates New York Harbor, slipping past the Statue of Liberty—*Liberty Enlightening the World.*

It's his second trip to the United States from Italy. The first was thirteen years before when he was a young immigrant of fifteen. Now a grown son, a hardworking and prosperous man, and a young father, he returns to the home he's made for himself.

Gulls swoop and dive as they trail the ship, hoping for a piece of bread or a bit of meat. The steamer's decks pulse with anxious travelers, the smell redolent of damp wool and fervent dreams. All day, they gather at the rails and chat in Yiddish, German, Russian, Armenian, Danish, Gaelic, and Italian while watching the green copper Lady come into view. Dominick, quiet and reverent, lifts his gray fedora, greeting once more the Lady who first welcomed him all those years ago.

He'd visited his parents back in Italy on this trip. It was the first time he'd been back since leaving Palo del Colle, his hometown in the province of Bari, in 1908. In the time he'd been gone, he'd married Nicoletta Troiano (a young girl also from Palo del Colle), and they'd had two children. He'd been an American for three years.

In this way, he was different from his father, a proud Italian. He was lucky, his father would tell him. When *he* was a boy, his father would note, the Risorgimento—the "rising again" that defined the creation of the Kingdom of Italy out of the minor kingdoms of the peninsula—was still in its infancy. To call oneself an Italian was, well, a magical, prideful honor. His father kept a portrait of that newly rising politician, Benito Mussolini, on the kitchen wall, not far from the crucifix. "That Mussolini . . . he understands what it means to be Italian."

Returning to America, Dominick had taken the swaddled cutting from the fig tree that shaded his parents' garden. Staring at the soon-to-be-transplanted cutting, he thought of his father, grandfathers, and great-grandfathers. Like them, he would strip the thin bark from one end of the branch and jab it into the soil at the home he and his wife had created far from the twisted olive trees, the braying donkeys, and the calamitous consequences—death by famine, for example, or malaria—of the poverty surrounding Palo del Colle.

He knows just the place to plant the seedling in the tiny yard behind their dun-colored house, just outside the little garden labyrinth where Nicoletta grows her roses. After docking, he'll make his way to the subway, to the solid house on Beverly Road in Brooklyn where he and Nicoletta have made a home.

In his hands he holds both the past and the future, the seeds carrying potential for him; his wife, Nicoletta; and their children. And through this rude transplantation, he will secure his place in the new land.

THE BOY WHO GOT AWAY

I don't often think of my grandfather, Dominick, but when I do, it's usually when I'm trying to remember who I am. Sometimes, all it takes to ground me is to remember his scent: a combination of Old Spice aftershave, the lanolin of his wool trousers, and the sweat of a man who provided for his children, his grandchildren, and his parents and in-laws—in both Palo del Colle and Brooklyn—by lugging blocks of ice up and down the stoops of Flatbush.

Remembering, I am transported back in time to when my

cheek would rub against his cheek as I burrowed my way into the crook of his neck, turning away from my mother and father and the chaos of their lives and into the safety of my grandparents' pale green kitchen, with its wall-mounted coffee grinder and the photo of Jesus baring his sacred heart, with eyes that followed you around the room. In the cool dark of the hallway just beyond Jesus was the pale green pantry with Stella D'oro cookies and the tin of lemon drops. Grandpa loved his lemon drops. And I loved Grandpa, so I loved his lemon drops.

In the swirl of such memories, I hear Nicoletta, my grandmother, whispering the rosary, serenaded by the soft *click-click, click-click, click-click* of beads sliding from one finger to the next as she counted off prayers for sins I can't ever imagine her having committed.

Freshly ground coffee simmers in the gurgling battered pot on the white enamel stove. Seated at the greenish Formica table with the rounded, chrome legs, holding a rubber band–bound stack of funerary prayer cards from the dozens of her relatives who've passed, she prays to ensure their reunion with God and their welcome home to heaven. Now and then, she glances at the portrait of Padre Pio, just below the Jesus with the roving eyes. Padre Pio mournfully watches over the kitchen while his hands are wrapped, the wraps bloody from the stigmata of the crucified Christ. The picture hangs near the wall-mounted black Bakelite rotary telephone. Grandma seeks his intercession to help with those heavenly aspirations of her relatives. Someday, she thinks, she'll need his help as well, especially given all the sins she's imagined she's committed. While some in the Church aren't happy with the devotion to Padre Pio, those from Palo del Colle know he was sent by God himself to those whom the world seemed to have abandoned.

Two images of my grandmother merge. In one, she is a girl of sixteen, a young woman in a lacy wedding dress, her arms linked with those of my eighteen-year-old grandfather, he in his very proper, very American suit. In the other, she is bent over that stack of prayer cards, her hair braided and tied over the crown of her head. I see the young bride in the elder grandmother. She is both the young bride and the grandmother who took her morning wine in a Welch's grape jelly jar. She especially liked the one with the cartoon of Fred Flintstone riding a brontosaurus, tossing his hard hat after a long day of work at the quarry.

Out the back door, just off the kitchen, is a porch where I would snag purple-black figs for their breakfast. The figs are for them, but picking the figs . . . well, that was my job.

Grandpa was a boy when he'd made his way to Brooklyn; his port of entry the immigration station at Castle Clinton, on the Battery, in lower Manhattan—just blocks from the enclave, the safety of Little Italy. He'd traveled third class— immigrant class—on the *Ancona*, a steamer named for the city on the Adriatic, north of Palo del Colle.

Imagining his story comforts me. I close my eyes and I see his first business: a pushcart in the streets of Little Italy. Maybe it was on Mott Street where the young boy of fifteen pushes his way through streets crowded with ladies in black dresses, their gray hair braided and knotted across the tops of their heads, gold crosses around their necks, maybe a touch of gold in their fillings.

From behind the cart, laden with blocks of ice covered with burlap and straw, I hear him crying out "Il ghiaccio! Il ghiaccio!"—"Ice! "Ice!"—next to the pushcarts with other young men offering to sharpen knives or sell you fresh fruit. Parking the pushcart in his cousin's garage on Delancey Street, he makes his way to Brooklyn, proud of having established himself as a man capable of sending money back home, putting a roof over his head, and someday bringing over his would-be wife, his Nicoletta, on another ship from Naples.

In my years in psychoanalysis, as I worked the stories of my childhood and tried to give some rest to the ghosts that haunted me, I came to think of myself as the *Boy Who Got Away*. The Boy Who Got Away from the chaos of a mentally ill mother, an alcoholic father, the shouting, the poverty. The Boy Who Got Away from violence in a house rooted in tensions stemming from mental illness that often pitted us kids against each other.

The violence within merged with the violence outside of our home. Outside were the tensions from economic and social injustices that pitted the children and grandchildren of immigrants against the grandchildren and great-grandchildren of enslaved people. Inside and out, the violence caused me to doubt my safety and, ultimately, my worthiness. Such conditions caused me to worry daily if I was safe, let alone worthy of love or Belonging.

Well into my adulthood I was haunted by such ghosts. It was only then that I began to understand how far I'd come, not only from the Flatbush, Brooklyn, of my childhood but also from the belief systems that defined and shaped who I thought I was supposed to be. Even now, as I think of the lives of my grandparents, I work to turn them from haunting ghosts into wise elders guiding me to the fullness of my adulthood.

Early on, when I first began altering those inherited belief systems, I clearly saw the negative effects of defining myself as the Boy Who Got Away. Yes, I was away. Yes, I was able to live my life free of the fears of violence and the shame of the poverty. But I also carried forward a guilt about who I'd left behind. Guilt, and grief for that which had been lost.

Now, as I consider the lives and loves, the wishes and dreams, the struggles and pains of my ancestors, I see Dominick Guido more clearly for who he was: the Original Boy Who Got Away. I wonder who and what he left behind. I am curious if he felt guilt or grief.

OUR ANCESTORS BEHIND US

I am never far from the little boy with a fresh crew cut whose head would be rubbed by Grandpa's rough, veined hands as we both enjoyed the sweet lemon drops he kept in that pale green pantry off the kitchen—the one with the sticky door that had to be yanked open.

While I am a man, and a good one at that, I will also always be that boy. While we are adults, we remain the children who prayed for Mom and Dad to stop fighting and for our home to be safe so that we might belong. Stuck at the top of the stairs as our parents forgot about us, we yearned to know that they saw us and, in seeing us, that we were loved.

As has been said of me often, I am the man who makes people cry. But it's not really me who makes folks cry. It's our memories that bring the tears. Those tears come because people struggle with their demons, the ghosts of those who came before, in the heartbreaking, heart-opening process of becoming the adults they were born to be. They struggle to grow up, to be better humans so that they can be better, happier leaders. And adults.

Clients, readers, those drawn to my work as a coach come to me because they struggle, they wish to change things, they wish to understand the ways they've been complicit, perhaps, in creating the conditions of their lives they say don't want.

Gently, compassionately, we use the tools of radical self-inquiry—the process by which the masks we hide behind, and the beliefs we hold that keep those masks in place, are slowly stripped away and revealed so there's no place—and no need—to hide. In doing so, we are slowly released from that which has happened to us so that we can then choose to be who we are to be. The psychologist Carl Jung once wrote that "I am not what has happened to me. I am what I choose to become."

To complete that process, to grow fully into the adult we were born to be, we must also be free of what happened to our ancestors. As hard as it is to release ourselves from the travails of our childhood, it's often harder to let go of what happened to those who came before us. For those who came before us, the agency of choosing what they will become may have been lost. Choosing who they are, choosing who they become, is our work to do. This is the work of descendants.

If being a better leader requires that we become better humans, being a better human requires that we become fully adult descendants. In doing so, we then have a chance of being ancestors, and not ghosts, to those who come after us.

VENERATING A LOST CAUSE

I have a friend who grew up in the American South. Like so many of his family and friends, he grew up with a profound respect for the past, a mythical reverence for the South's Lost Cause.

Indeed, in his home state of North Carolina, that past is venerated. But that veneration hides dark truths about his ancestors. They served the Confederacy. They supported North Carolina's secession from the Union in what he was taught was the War of Northern Aggression. The family stories also held that they had been poor farmers, too poor to have enslaved people.

But all that veneration, all that respect for the past, and the admiration of the sacrifices of his ancestors belie an equally important and far more troubling truth: they may not have directly enslaved people, but they benefited from the system that did. Moreover, as my friend discovered when he was going through some old newspaper clippings from his hometown, participation in that system made it easier for them to have enjoyed a picnic at the lynching of a Black man. He's seen the pictures that prove it.

For my friend, seeing the ghostly faces of his ancestors gathered around the hanging body of a Black man was shocking; their actions went against everything he believed about his family and, therefore, himself. But his commitment to creating the world he wants to see compelled him to no longer look away, to see that his ancestors were not merely noble, poor tenant farmers but also beneficiaries of a system of oppression that he is committed to dismantling. In order to further the world he wants to will into existence, he must see—and accept—the fullness of his ancestors' experiences, actions, and choices. In order for each of us to will a world of Belonging into existence, we must accept our ancestors' full stories, even the parts that might be reprehensible.

This is what it takes to become the ancestors our descendants deserve; we must each see—fully see—our ancestors.

This is the foundation we must unearth and sometimes rebuild to become the person, the adult, we were meant to be.

A PILLAR OF BELONGING

Growing toward such light, new stories emerge, moving us toward becoming the adults we were born to be, rising higher to the aspirational goal of leading while creating Belonging for ourselves and, more importantly, for those with whom we live, laugh, work, and love. We must become more than who our ancestors were. We must become the trees our ancestors traveled so far to plant in the soil of a new land. Such transgenerational transformation is necessary for us to be active co-conspirators in creating systemic and lasting Belonging.

You're right, Justin: Inclusivity *is* the felt sense of love, safety, and Belonging. But that transformation is complex and difficult. Cognitive awareness of our beliefs—rooted as they are in the experiences of our ancestors—is essential for this transformation; essential but, ultimately, insufficient.

We must augment that awareness with the beauty and art of a felt sense of who we are, where we have come from, and the ancestors whose lives we carry within us. We must not only feel our ancestors' hands on our backs but carry their pain, their failings, their heartbreaks, their dreams, and their resilience. We must remember who they were and not merely what the family legends tell us they were. When we do this, when we *reunite* with the reality of who they were, we transform our ancestors from unknown, unseen, unrecognized ghosts who haunt us into ancestors who accompany us, hands on our backs, steadying us as we face the inevitable and necessary struggle known simply as growing up. We rescue them from what happened to them and help them to become what we choose them to be.

In bravely reuniting with our past, we turn their stories from the unreplicable and mysterious achievements of super-humans into relatable acts of courage and human frailty. Then, in a bit of alchemy, they become a source of strength, pillars of our own Belonging upon which we may then build a house of Belonging for others.

Like paper cranes laid next to the etched names of ghosts, our family stories, collective memories, and even the family secrets form a mythology around our beginning and, there-fore, our Belonging. Exploring our origin myths, looking into the secrets that maintain the mythology, turns our ghosts into ancestors. Knowing from whom we are descended, knowing the places they walked and the air they breathed, knowing the rich experiences of their lives reunites us with the past. Such reunifications give meaning to the present while guiding us toward a future of full actualization.

Who are your ancestors? What were the stories you were told about them? What subroutines and belief systems do those stories reveal of their lives and their journeys? What might the tales of resilience and overcoming of adversity say about the underlying beliefs of those who might want to mi-grate for a better life?

Our lineage, and the tales told in support of the origin myths, shape how we respond to the world. If our task is to create and sustain Belonging, to break through our silent com-plicity in systemic Othering, we need to see the connection between the experience of those around us and those of our ancestors. My grandmother anxiously waiting for my grand-father to receive her at Ellis Island is not all that different from the mother from Guatemala at the southern border of the United States, anxiously hoping that the long journey from home will keep her children safe.

Be warned, though. While understanding who our ancestors were makes their love palpable and their journeys real, while it may justify our present-day realities of privilege, such knowledge is costly. When we look to the places they lived and loved, cried and died, we may tear the fabricated memories that have comforted us, shredding the gauze of myth through which we view the past and our ancestors. Reunion requires that we see our ancestors not as we wish to see them, not through a gauze that softens and thereby distorts, but as they really were.

CHAPTER 2

The Gauze of Myth

We are what we pretend to be, so we must be
careful about what we pretend to be.

—KURT VONNEGUT, *MOTHER NIGHT*

It's a conundrum. We often know our families and their pasts only through the myths our elders tell and the stories we pretend are true. In our elders' embrace, we're nurtured and nourished by that which they choose to share, that which we are allowed to know. We're often confounded by what we pretend is true.

Safely wrapped in my grandfather's arms, I was soothed by the scent of Old Spice and lemon drops. I connected to a dreamy, fabricated memory of Palo del Colle. In his arms, I pretended myself into the tiny painting of the port of Bari that hung in my grandparents' living room.

I imagined myself on the dock as gulls dart overhead, ladies in black dresses sit beside that morning's drying pasta, and men who look like Grandpa and his father and his father before him stand next to that morning's catch; a squid writhes in anticipation, perhaps, of being a meal with that pasta on the rack. I knew that I had never really lived there, yet, still, I would stare into that painting and swear that I would one day return "home" to where I belonged. I dreamed up memories of my life in the fig tree grove outside my great-grandparents' home. Even today, when I sit still enough, I can hear the wind in the leaves of those imagined trees. In Grandpa's arms, no matter how much my parents' struggles made my home unsafe, I knew to whom I belonged. Knowing that, I thought, I knew how to belong to myself.

"The greatest thing in the world is knowing how to belong to oneself," wrote philosopher Michel de Montaigne. Indeed, amid the chaos of my youngest days, I could dream into existence my home, the rooms to which I belonged, in Palo del Colle. In the quiet of my bedroom, I could belong to myself.

Still, the conundrum. It stems from the inadequacy and insufficiencies of such fabricated memories. It confounds. If that Belonging to myself is based on fabrications, can I trust the feeling? If my Belonging even to myself depends on the myths that my family shared like the pasta passed around the table, to whom and to where do I *really* belong?

Experiencing the truth of our ancestors requires that we rip the gauzy mythology of their having overcome trials and withstood tribulations, of romantic ideals of immigrant resilience. To be held up by this first pillar, to turn ghosts into ancestors with hands on our backs, we must deconstruct their myths. We must see our parents, grandparents, and great-grandparents as flesh and bone, with hearts as easily broken as our own. This is the cost that we pay to extract an adult sense of Belonging from the fabricated memories.

More importantly, the price of this ticket is seeing what we don't want to see and knowing what we have not wanted to know. The price will be that we can no longer pretend to be what we are not.

WHY DIDN'T I KNOW THIS?

Jason's most pronounced characteristics are his eclectic interests in things like physics, hunting, photography, and building companies. His beard is often scraggly, and he's got a booming, big laugh. He can laugh at the absurdity of life in a start-up, and he aims the biggest laughs at himself. I adore his laughter.

My client for just over a year, he's like me. He, too, traces his family back to Italy. Most of his family came from the north, though. It was a scandal, then, when one of his ancestors married a boy from the south, from Sicily. The Sicilian grandfather had somehow overstepped centuries-old boundaries and married "up."

We were speaking about the effects of family lineage on our current lives, we were talking about the stories, the myths, and the beliefs formed in response to the events of our ancestors' lives and the way they become the basis for the subroutines undergirding our leadership and our lives. "Ghosts in the machine," I once described them, the invisible, unspoken-of forces that run our lives; the subroutines that define the rules by which we live.

I shared a bit of the work I was doing for this book. I shared about the poverty our ancestors faced in Italy. We shared stories we'd heard as children about life back there, back in Italy. We laughed and enjoyed the gauze that is the myth.

But the mood shifted when I began sharing some of the facts of the experience of our grandparents and great-grandparents in becoming white, in becoming Americans. I had opened the box of those experiences by sharing my own discomfort, and our laughter was silenced. He blurted out, "Why didn't I know this?" when I noted that, in 1891, in New Orleans, a mob broke into the jail and went after nineteen Italian immigrants being held accused of murdering a white man, an American (as the press styled it), the police chief David Hennessy.

After the jury acquitted the men, but before they were released, a mob broke into the jail and shot some "like curs" (wrote one paper). Others they clubbed to death. Eleven of the acquitted were then dragged out and hanged by the mob.

"These sneaking and cowardly Sicilians," wrote the editors at the *New York Times* after the hanging, "the descendants of bandits and assassins, who have transported to this country the lawless passions, the cut-throat practices, and the oath-bound societies of their native country, are to us a pest without mitigations. Our own rattlesnakes are as good citizens as they are."

When I read that quote it sounded familiar. I thought back to 2015 when then-candidate Donald Trump announced his presidential run. "When Mexico sends its people, they're not sending their best," the future president declared. "They're not sending you. They're not sending you. They're sending people that have lots of problems, and they're bringing those problems with us. They're bringing drugs. They're bringing crime. They're rapists. And some, I assume, are good people."*

"You and me," I said to Jason after I'd shared the quote from the *Times*. "You and me, Jason . . . we're descendants of bandits, assassins, and rattlesnakes," I said. Neither of us laughed. After a pause, he repeated more to himself than to me, "Why didn't I know this?"

---

* "Donald Trump's False Comments Connecting Mexican Immigrants and Crime," *Washington Post*, July 8, 2015, https://www.washington post.com/news/fact-checker/wp/2015/07/08/donald-trumps-false -comments-connecting-mexican-immigrants-and-crime/.

What else didn't we know? What else did we pretend wasn't true? We didn't know that, after the New Orleans murders, a young civil service commissioner wrote his sister of a dinner he'd had with "various dago diplomats" who were "all much wrought up by the lynching of the Italians in New Orleans." He closed that section of his letter with, "Personally, I think it rather a good thing, and said so." The commissioner was Theodore Roosevelt.

"Why didn't either of us know any of these things?" I answered him. Why didn't well-informed, well-educated, and highly privileged men like us know that the horrific internment of some three hundred thousand Americans of Japanese descent included a much, much smaller, but rarely acknowledged, contingent of thousands of Americans of Italian and German descent.

There's no equivalency between the internments of these groups. The racism Japanese Americans faced must be viewed within the larger context of the overall alienation and Othering they faced as immigrants and the children of immigrants from Japan. This, in addition to the long-lived and continuing anti-Asian racism manifested in laws excluding those from China from immigrating to the States, a racism that to this day remains uncomfortably, painfully, heartbreakingly unacknowledged, rearing up occasionally when their collective Otherness is used as justification for scapegoating, as what happened early in the COVID pandemic.

But why wasn't the post–Pearl Harbor attack roundup part of the family myths that our families told to one another around the Sunday-afternoon dinner tables? What didn't we collectively want to know about the thousands of our ancestors' compatriots who were rounded up during the night of December 7,

1941—questioned, detained, relocated, and, for some, interned because the country that took them in considered them aliens? Despite the declared intentions of men such as my grandfather, they were not, after all, American. Overnight, they were once more unmitigated pests. The enemy. The Other.

Rattlesnakes.

"We have people coming into the country—or trying to come in—we're stopping a lot of them," Trump told reporters two years after the comment about Mexican immigrants. "You wouldn't believe how bad these people are. These aren't people, these are animals."*

Animals.

Dehumanization is a pillar of systemic Othering. And for such dehumanization to take hold, those who've assimilated must forget the oppression, the Othering, of their ancestors. This is how those who were Othered are complicit in, and benefit from, the Othering of others.

WHY CAN'T THEY ASSIMILATE LIKE WE DID?

Grandpa's journey to becoming an American included more than identifying himself as an "American Italian," more than identifying with the forces that controlled whether or not he would be accepted or continued to be perceived as alien, foreign, an "other." It included his, and the family's, willful disregard of facts such as these.

---

* "Trump Calls Some Undocumented Immigrants 'Animals' in a Rant," *New York Times*, May 16, 2018, https://www.nytimes.com/2018/05/16 /us/politics/trump-undocumented-immigrants-animals.html.

It included, perhaps, even cultivating ignorance of the suffering of others as much as a rejection of teaching his children Barese, the dialect of his childhood, the dialect of his ancestors. Like so many others in so many realms, to be safe, my ancestors identified as white Americans, despite those who questioned whether they belonged here and charged that they should go back to where they came from.

"We had both grown up hearing things like 'we were nothing but a bunch of guineas to the *'mericani*' and 'why can't these immigrants assimilate like we did?'" write Jennifer Guglielmo and Salvatore Salerno in their book *Are Italians White?* "Self-righteousness and blame were a way the Italians around us continually distinguished themselves from people of color. The collective memory of oppression, it seemed, was rarely used to fight racism and challenge systemic inequality."

Rarely used, perhaps, because to acknowledge the memories of the Othering of our ancestors would mean our collective hold on acceptance and Belonging would be revealed to be tenuous, fleeting, ephemeral, withdrawn the minute one group member steps out of line. Indeed, that hard-won acceptance can suddenly be withdrawn because some politician in some far-off government makes some far-off decision or dares to question American exceptionalism.

Or, as in the aftermath of the terrorist attacks on 9/11, turbaned Sikh men were attacked for not being from "here"—however indeterminate being "from here" is—because people blame those who appear different and in that difference seem just like those who threatened us. Whoever "they" are. Whoever "we" are. This "us" is nothing more than a construct of minds influenced far too easily by those who seek the power enabled by division.

Indeed, the lives of the families we construct, the communities with which we identify, are built on myths, half-truths, and stories we repeat to comfort ourselves. The men and women we model ourselves after are crafted from the stories we tell sitting around and, as in my case, under the tables where we gather. The pasta and squid being passed around with stories of our successful assimilation and the casual observations that those who now struggle to belong should just "assimilate like we did."

Equal parts legend and fact, the stories of and about our ancestors are crafted from the facts we pretend to be true as well as the deletions and distortions that make our ancestors either someone to oppose ("I'll never be like them!") or to emulate ("If only I could be half the man that he was."). Family stories, and the subroutines that reinforce and maintain them, are crafted as much by what we choose *not* to know as by what we choose to remember.

For example, those who look like me often choose to overlook how our ancestors assimilated. The myths we tell ourselves leave little room for the Faustian bargains struck, enabling us to move from alien to accepted. The dark-skinned, racially inferior *meridionali* became the safe, white American. Moreover, such privileges were afforded to me because my ancestors were granted a thin, quick, take-it-before-it-disappears chance to assimilate into the majority culture. No longer the Other, Grandpa became an American; the safety of Belonging in America seemingly worth all that may have been lost. Lost language, lost culture, and even lost connections with those left behind. The *Boy Who Got Away* left not only the land but all that was, all that may have defined home, hearth, and the sources of Belonging.

HOW HAVE I BENEFITED FROM THE SUFFERING OF OTHERS?

One of the foundational moves of my work as a leadership coach is to ask my clients to consider how they might have been complicit in creating the conditions they say they don't want. That question, first taught to me by my now-passed psychoanalyst Dr. Avivah Sayres, transformed my life. Questions like that, turned over for nearly thirty years as I lay on Dr. Sayres's couch, staring at that damned ceiling, wondering if she'd fallen asleep, helped me see the subtle forces at work that maintained the dissatisfaction, the discomfort, and the depression of my life.

But when one seeks relief from the subroutines and negative belief systems that hold us back from becoming the fully actualized adults we were born to be; when one turns the lens of analytic inquiry inward, the ego will defend itself by throwing up shame as flak to confuse the heat-seeking missiles of radical self-inquiry.

When working with a client, then, I must quickly point out that complicit means they are an *accomplice*. They are complicit, I'll say, but not entirely *responsible*; this way, they don't absorb entirely the shame-producing guilt that can arise when we begin to see more clearly the conditions of our lives. I add that such conditions all too often represent what we consciously say we don't want but nevertheless, because of the subroutine beliefs of our ancestors, we unconsciously maintain.

The explorations into the "wreck" of our lives and, as poet

Adrienne Rich writes in her brilliant work *Diving into the Wreck*, not the stories of the wreck, are essential to the radical self-inquiry necessary for the transformation, the adulting, the growing up into our fullest selves—the goal we desperately seek.

Now, beyond my own growth into adulthood, I have a responsibility to look to the larger, outer world. I must look beyond the wreck itself. I know that when we seek to turn the unremembered ghosts of our past into ancestors who accompany us on our journey into creating the world we want to see exist, we are called to evolve that basic question. Viewed through the wider lens of lineage and the true experience of our ancestors as well as those with whom we live, work, build communities, and raise children, the question expands to encompass more than my own experience. The question becomes, How have I been complicit in, and benefited from, the conditions of Othering I say I don't want to exist?

Leaders—indeed, all those who hold power—must be willing to face such questions with the same fearless, broken-open warrior hearts with which they radically inquire within. To do otherwise means they are using their power to maintain the systems that not only hold back others but also Othered their ancestors. Systemic Othering isn't bound by constructs of race or place. It's not even bound by time. It is a force that must be confronted daily.

I couldn't answer Jason's question about why he hadn't known this, why this wasn't part of the family myths for so many of the descendants of the Italian immigrants. In the moment, I felt only kinship. I hadn't known either. But slowly, as I used the tools of radical self-inquiry and expanded their application into an inquiry into the lives of my ancestors, I began to understand why the status of the refuge seekers at the southern border of the United States, or those stuck in airports, denied entry because the dominant religious beliefs of their home country followed the teachings of Islam, doesn't evoke universal compassion.

In choosing to be American, in allowing ourselves to be racialized as white, in choosing the safety of the dominant class, too many of us gave up the knowledge of what our ancestors suffered and, as a result, diminished our capacity for collective compassion; such compassion is crucial to reunion. It's as if the pain of having been abandoned even by Christ the Redeemer makes us all abandoners.

CHRIST STOPPED AT EBOLI

There's a dark, sad saying that can still resonate in the southern reaches of Italy; in Puglia, Calabria, and Salerno, if you listen to the old ones, the ones who remember when malaria was a daily threat, when a smoked fish hung over a fire dripped and the juices caught between slices of bread constituted a meal, or when the olive harvests would fail and the grandmothers would make the pasta from bran instead of semolina, making even the orecchiette dry and hard to swallow, "Christ," they say, "stopped at Eboli." Christ, they mean, doesn't descend farther south than Eboli. Those south of, and surrounding the commune of Eboli, were left to fend for themselves.

In the middle to late nineteenth century, as various forces battled to unify the minor kingdoms and city-states of the peninsula, there was an effort to identify and classify the peoples of that land. Those in southern provinces such as Puglia—the land of my ancestors—were regarded as racially, genetically inferior to those in the north—those who shared culture, language, and beliefs about the Christ. This perceived inferiority mirrored the "modern science" of eugenics rising in America and beyond, classifying people into races and barring entry to many.

In Italy, this Othering was evidenced not only by my ancestors' perceived cultural backwardness but by their poverty. Like far too many peoples of the world, my people were othered, shamed, denigrated precisely because they were poor, which was seen as a reason for Othering and not its consequence.

The "racially inferior" southern Italians believed that they, the *meridionali*, were abandoned, left bereft by the God they dutifully worshipped because they were undeserving. No, for the *meridionali*, there was just Padre Pio. As with so many who are systemically oppressed, my ancestors internalized the oppression and believed the lie of their unworthiness—their lives unredeemable even by the redeemer Himself.

Even the princes of that region, such as Prince Colonna di Stigliano, would spend more time in Rome than in Stigliano, in Matera, in the ancient Basilicata peopled originally by immigrants from Greece and, so says the myth, Troy.

My father's father, Vito Jerome Colonna, told stories of such princes of the south, subtly referencing Prince Colonna in such a way that I, as a little boy, imagined myself a long-lost prince, just waiting to be found. Found, rescued, and reunited with my princely family. I pretended to be royalty.

Christ's abandonment of the south marked my ancestors and, as is the way with all such ancient, intergenerational traumas, found footing in the minds of their descendants; descendants like me. When you travel to escape home; when you leave behind parents, siblings, cousins, the blood of your blood; when you abandon your language, the smells and sights that define your land, and the bones of your grandparents and their parents and their grandparents—all for the chance to eat the fish and not just the fish-flavored slices of bread—when you leave all, when you leave the father who brought you forth, the mother who nursed you despite her own starvation, who are you but the one who also abandons?

Perhaps, deep in your heart, as you watch the waves crash against the steamer taking you across an unfathomably vast ocean to a new world, you are convinced that you are just another example of that distortion of the Christ message: you are Christ the Abandoner. Perhaps then, as the smell of the salt air mixes with diesel fumes, you consider the future and vow to be like the other Christ, the one the priests at the Chiesa di San Giuseppe in Palo del Colle preached about, the Redeemer. You swear that you will be the one who comes back, comes back and takes care of those you left behind. You swear you will redeem them.

WRITING THAT BEGINS IN THE BLOOD

In *Reboot*, where I used the process of my own radical self-inquiry to explore the structures and subroutines of my childhood to unpack and understand my approaches to adulthood and leadership, I undertook a process as a model for how those with whom I work might explore their own stories. In doing so, I ended up grappling with my feelings of shame and guilt. After diving into the wreck of my childhood, I surfaced as an adult, reasonably convinced that, through it all, I emerged a good man.

This exploration has been equally, if differently, challenging.

First, there is the experience of being in the liminal space between conscious thought and unconscious feelings. Writing about my ancestors lit my brain on fire. I found myself waking from dreams of olive trees and braying donkeys, of malaria and famine.

"It's from that place that great writing comes," my therapist assured me after hearing my nightmares. "The writing begins," he went on, paraphrasing Rainer Maria Rilke, "in the blood."

"All the soarings of my mind," Rilke wrote, "begin in my blood."

As I dove deep into the wreck of the lives of the immigrants who are my ancestors, the soarings of my mind led me to viscerally sense their wishes, their dreams, their fears, and even the sights, sounds, and smells of their journeys. Many nights I lay awake in my bed, drenched in the sweat, perhaps, of my laborer ancestors. My brain was on fire, and my blood lit up with what I can only describe as an intergenerational, transpersonal transference.

These soarings, these wake-me-from-the-dead-of-night-with-cold-sweats dream states, these wreck dives into the lives of my ancestors began in my blood. Their stories became my wordless, viscerally felt stories. I realized that for these soarings to have any value, to contribute anything to my own wishes to belong and to support the quest to help others create systemic Belonging, they must continue to be sourced in my blood.

In the past, I wrote of Grandpa's lemon drops. The candies became more than a metaphor for the love, safety, and Belonging I felt at his house. They became a stand-in for my pursuit of safety that money seemed to offer. As I came to understand his life even more, though, I was struck by the irony of my own projection: Grandpa, who to me represented the safety of wealth, had been reared in a place and time of bitter poverty and attendant shame.

Dreaming of the Othering of my ancestors, I descended into a depression. Then suddenly everything shifted. That depression, and the overwhelmed psyche that accompanied it, was relieved on James Baldwin's birthday.

On that day, social media was flooded with Baldwin quotes. As I endeavored to explore the moral obligations of leaders to create systems of Belonging, I was drawn to Baldwin's teachings. One quote stood out: "When you're writing," he told the *New York Times* in an interview, "you're trying to find out something which you don't know. The whole language of writing for me is finding out what you don't want to know, what you don't want to find out. But something forces you to anyway."

WHAT DIDN'T I WANT TO FIND OUT?

Writing in fits and starts, what was it that I didn't want to find out? And, more, what was it that forced me forward regardless?

As with all well-asked questions, the answer became clearer the more I probed the question. I didn't want to find out just how unwelcome my ancestors were. I didn't want to understand that there was a time when they were considered nonwhite and, because of the racist structure that has always been a part of this country, therefore unworthy of Belonging. They were rejected by a society that has a well-documented, indisputable history of pulling up the drawbridge after the last of "our" people, the acceptable people, have made it aboard, denying Belonging to others who are in the same position that we were in just moments before. Think of the presidential candidate descending a glitzy escalator after declaring that those who came to this land across the imaginary border—a line drawn in the sand, valleys, and hills on the edge of this country—were rapists and criminals, despite his own ancestors' crossing of the Atlantic, seeking the same Belonging; as the supremacist powers that be declared, pests without mitigations. Dehumanized rattlesnakes. Animals seeking shelter.

We do it to immigrants. We do it to the poor. We do it to anyone and everyone whose success seems to threaten us. We are crabs in buckets, scrambling to both get out and not be pulled down by those who remain stuck on the bottom. This despite the impulse to drag down, drag back anyone who has the temerity to climb out, reject the confines of shame, poverty, and our own Otherness.

In southern Italy, folks will say of anyone who tries to be educated, to leave the confines of the neighborhood, to go beyond the cloistered walls of family, to step beyond the communes of Puglia, Campania, Calabria, or Basilicata that "they think they're too big." The sin is in thinking oneself worthy of escaping the bucket, of being deserving of Belonging.

I'm reminded of a client who one day faced severe backlash from her colleagues. After months of trying to get my client, the CEO of her company, to address what her colleagues were asserting was the structural racism at the company, her employees—all ten of them—quit. As dedicated as they were to the work, work that involved helping other companies address systemic inequities, they could no longer afford to, no longer stand working for, my client's company.

The employees' chief complaint was that they were severely underpaid. "I treated them like my students," said my client, who had a long and successful career as a coach and facilitator. "I feel betrayed," she added. "I gave them all opportunities."

"Is there any basis for their objection?" I asked my client. "No," she said, "the internships were paid."

After some further unpacking, including a detailed exploration of her profit and loss statement, I said, "So your entire business is built on the assumption of low or unpaid labor."

From where I sit, as a former investor and venture capitalist, businesses that depend on unpaid labor may seem profitable, I told her, but they are, in fact, terribly fragile businesses. "Even unethical," I added.

Her stunned reexamination of her business model led eventually to an even further conclusion. Probing with intuition, I asked for more details about how she came to the career she'd come to. Quickly, we arrived at her ancestors.

"They were from Virginia," she said flatly.

"So they were farmers?" I asked.

"In a sense . . . they grew tobacco. For generations."

"*Who* grew the tobacco?" I asked, emphasizing the word *who*.

She paused as the echo of her ancestors' complicity in, and benefit from, slavery caught up to her.

The true story of her ancestors' experience was shielded from her consciousness by the family version of the myth of exceptionalism and resilience. They weren't plantation owners; they were farmers who pulled themselves up by their bootstraps. The myth, as it does collectively for the country, shielded the family from the truth they didn't want to know.

Despite such gauzy myths, of course, dark shadows of extractive capitalism and the enslavement of others never really leaves us.

One night, at a recent boot camp, the attendees had gathered into a spontaneous fireside chat. I had read a bit from this book, the manuscript very much still a work in progress. I had read that passage, the one about the former client and her slaveholding ancestors.

Jaime stopped me just after we broke and were getting ready for dinner. He had tears in his eyes.

"Jerry," he said, "I'm having a kind of out-of-body experience." He went on to tell me that he had been born in the Dominican Republic and immigrated to New York fourteen years earlier. Since then, he'd developed a successful career in advertising. But the thing he wanted to share at that moment was related to why he'd come to the boot camp. "Jerry," he continued, "I have struggled all my life with guilt. Guilt and shame." He paused and then continued. "I think I know why now."

"My great-grandmother had been a slave," he shared through tears. "She was raped by my great-grandfather. And my grandfather was the result."

Laid before me, through those tears, was the guilt, perhaps, of his great-grandfather and the shame (undeserving as it might be) of his great-grandmother.

Listening deeply to my ancestors, I said forcefully, "You've got to find out her name."

He struggled. He stammered. "My father doesn't know who she was. We don't talk about her."

"I didn't say you had to ask your father her name," I challenged him with a fierceness that surprised me. "I said *you* have to find out her name." You must remember her, I told him.

We must remember all of them. Like me, Jaime benefited in the grand canard called race. Like my client, to be identified as part of a dominant group meant to have benefited from the Othering of everyone else.

What is it that we choose not to remember? What do we not want to take in? That our ancestors and their compatriots were, and may continue to be, complicit in maintaining the conditions that we, their descendants, say we don't want to see in the world.

MAKING OTHERS

When I was thirteen, my family moved from one part of Brooklyn—Flatbush—to another—Bensonhurst. We moved from an area increasingly populated by Black Americans who, as part of the Great Northward Migration from the South, joined the Black population whose roots in Brooklyn predated the arrival of my ancestors.

We moved to an area where the children and grandchildren of *meridionali* immigrants dominated the classrooms, the pizzerias, the streets, and the chain-link-fence-bounded schoolyards and playgrounds. It was an area where the collective memory of oppression was not only rarely used as a way to fight racism but, rather, as a means to justify it.

Just blocks from where my friends and I prowled the streets of Bensonhurst, Yusef Hawkins was beaten and shot by a gang of Italian American kids simply for being in the wrong neighborhood. Looking to buy a used car, Hawkins had crossed the imaginary border between Coney Island and Bensonhurst.

It was the summer between elementary school and high school when my friends met at Mario's Pizzeria on Avenue T, played some pinball, and started toward the schoolyard. As we got nearer to McDonald Avenue, one friend, Sal, started complaining about the Jews—Hasidim—who lived on the other side of McDonald. "Our neighborhood," he said. "Stupid hats," he said. "Weird clothes," he said. "They smell," he said.

"Let's beat up some Jews," he said. Everyone went quiet. Stevie kicked the ground. Paulie, always with a Spaldeen in his hands, nervously threw the ball in the air and caught it, over and over.

"Fuck this," I said, not brave enough to say what I really felt—that this was wrong, that this was stupid, that this wasn't right. I turned toward home and Sal yelled: "Pussy!"

I stopped, turned, and leaped at him, causing us both to fly into the air. We landed with me on top and smashing his face. I still remember the feeling of his nose crunching under my fist. I remember Stevie and Paulie, both twice my size, struggling to pull me off him. "You're going to kill him."

Where did my rage come from? Like so many boys, the threat of having my masculinity challenged was terrifying, but while threat of being a "wuss" or a "pussy" was intense, looking back, I think my rage was deeper even than the risk of some boyish notion of manliness. The risk to which I responded with rage was a deep-rooted suffering born out of not knowing to whom and to where I belonged.

Like my ancestors before, perhaps I was fighting the impotence of not Belonging. Impotence and suffering. The writer Parker Palmer, my teacher and friend, says that violence is what we do when we don't know what to do with our suffering. My violence, the violence of young boys on a street at night, and even Sal's violence all stem from the same impotent rage against systems of non-Belonging: the violence we visit upon each other, the smashing of the other's safety, born out of our own insecure grasp on Belonging.

Revisiting that story now, I reexperienced the shame of having taken so long to stand against such Othering. Making Others out of the rest of the world, those not from our neighborhood or, worse, those who simply didn't conform, was an everyday practice in the worlds I inhabited. For as strange as Sal was, I struggle to accept the truth that he wasn't an anomaly. He was normal. He was like the rest of us. He thought nothing of making fun of someone for little more than their differences.

Like my ancestors before me, far too often we remain silent when our friends and peers denigrate anyone who doesn't look, talk, walk like them. Or anyone who doesn't fit the model of who or what we were supposed to be. Like Paulie B. tossing the Spaldeen high in the air over and over, I would look away. I would choose not to see. To belong, I chose not to see things. We chose to remain silent.

I never said anything, for example, when the young girl who lived across from us on West Seventh Street was continually tormented because she had been misgendered at birth. I remember her vividly. At thirteen, she was sorting out her identity. She'd walk home from the local middle school with a gang of girls. You could hear them laughing and talking from far away. Then someone would hurl something at her— usually words but oftentimes a rock, a stick, a Spaldeen. She may have angrily flipped a bird at Paulie B. when, sitting on the front steps of my house, he called her horrible names. She may have told him to "fuck off," as only a kid from Brooklyn could do. But from the corner of my eye, and behind my guarded heart, I would sometimes look more closely, see her and her heart, and watch as she ran home crying. I may not have participated in the attacks, but my silence was complicity.

Like our ancestors, we chose to identify with the oppressor. I, too, didn't access the collective memory of oppression and suffering. It was too risky. I was more often silent in the making of Others than the adult version of me wants to admit. This, too, was what I didn't want to know but was forced to write.

It's hard to look to the things we don't want to know. But I know of no other way to induce further growth, to expand into our commitments not only to be adult leaders but to use our power and privilege (hard gained by our ancestors) to manifest the world we know needs to be.

Looking at what I didn't want to know, I come to a new question: What was lost after my grandfather made *his* choice? When he chose to be an American?

The Palo del Colle of my family's stories is wrapped in the romantic, whispery gauze of yearnings. Despite having visited my grandparents' hometown, I have no sense of the reality of the place. My ancestors' pursuit of Belonging left me with an inheritance of more than white privilege. It also left me with myths and stories that, when viewed only through the gauze of legend, are myths, stories of who we are, and where and to whom we belong. A place that looms large in the myths of immigration, Ellis Island was the ostensible gateway to Belonging, but it was also a place of separation and Othering. To fit in, to belong, the myth of who we were, and ultimately who we are, was created so that we would be distanced from the realities of what our ancestors experienced.

What they experienced and what continues to be experienced even today. When a border patrol agent on horseback, working the southern border of the United States, seems to use their reins to whip and chase a refuge-seeking immigrant from Haiti who has crossed many borders to come to the United States, our collective memories of oppression are ignored and not used to fight systemic racism. In such ignorance, we fail to see that their story—the story of the refugee seeking safety—is our ancestors' story. Their stories are our stories. "Your story is my story," indeed.

We must move past myths and take in the complicated and conflicting realities of the starving, oppressed, "huddled masses" who then benefited from the very system that would have excluded them. If we don't remember our ancestors' experiences, our perceptions of those at the southern border will, at best, remain gauzily trapped in sympathetic pitying and, at worst, antagonistically threatening. I cannot be empathetic to their longing to belong until I allow myself to reunite with the trauma of my ancestors' struggles.

I think of my friend Bijan, a former venture capitalist and now ambassador to the Czech Republic. We spoke shortly after the ban on travel from predominantly Muslim countries was chaotically and cruelly implemented. Witnessing that, he was brought back to 1979, when the Shah of Iran was overthrown, the Islamic Republic of Iran was declared, and the US embassy in Tehran was seized. Suddenly he went from being the boy playing Wiffle ball with his friends in the waning sunlight of a Long Island summer's eve to the Other; his father is Persian.

I think, too, of my friend Leslie, whose ancestors escaped the Nazi pogroms and immigrated to Costa Rica. We spoke during some of the most virulent anti-immigrant actions of modern days, and Leslie—who has dedicated her work life to helping those on the margins of entrepreneurial success—was questioning when she truly belonged here, in the country where she was raising her children.

We honor our ancestors by seeing as much of them as possible. We honor them by taking in the ways their experiences shape our lives now. To be a worthy descendant and ancestor, I must root into the humus of the decomposing dreams and wishes, as well as the challenges to my ancestors' love, safety, and Belonging. My own sense of Belonging remains tenuous until I know and experience such suffering. For as long as our own sense of Belonging remains tenuous—consciously and unconsciously, wittingly or not—we threaten the Belonging of others. Reuniting with the truth of who they were makes that verb, *reunite*, active and present tense. In so doing, it exemplifies the implicit process. When I reunite with who they were, I move one step closer toward my own wholeness.

As I seek to foster systemic Belonging, I must look to the things I do not want to see but about which I am forced to write: How have we been complicit in, and benefited from, the conditions in the world, in our communities, and among the people we claim to love that we say we do not want to exist? And, more, what do we have to give up that we love and value—including perceptions of ourselves as descended from princes—to create the systems of Belonging we want?

I can't tell you what Grandma's voice sounded like; it is too far in my distant memory. But I can tell you how she smelled (like roses, wine, and a sweetness that comes from praying constantly) and what the hem of the sleeve of her housedress felt like as I lay in her arms and twisted it over and over (and over) again. Such memories feel embedded in my genes.

BECOMING AN ANCESTOR

I am the fig-tree cutting of my ancestors' famine, their suffering, their journeys across oceans, their landings in a pursuit of
love, safety, and, most of all, Belonging. For they knew that if
they could belong, they would be safe. And if they were safe,
they could love and be loved. I am why they crossed an ocean,
endured the loss of place, put up with the shame and humili-
ation of being Othered. I am descended not from princes and
princesses who ruled by a power granted or stolen by the human tendency of separation and gradation. The princes and
princesses of my lineage are marked in sweat and toil, figs and
olives, and the willingness to risk whatever significance they
held for their descendants. In my quest to belong, I hope to
become a worthy descendant.

And, therefore, a loving ancestor to the future. I am the
branch that is replanted and rooted in new lands, dropping
fruit that will deliver seeds for new trees to sprout. I am the fruit
of all that they were and the choices they made. I am the fig
tree of my ancestors' dreams.

I am sheltered by my ancestors. Their myths sustained me.
Their lemon drops, figs, and fresh-ground coffee fed me. But
working to become an ancestor, their worthy descendant,
means moving beyond the myths and into the fullness of their
stories. For their stories are my stories just as my stories will be
the stories of my descendants.

When I no longer deny who they were, when I no longer
deny uncomfortable aspects of the past, I go beyond turning
them from ghosts into ancestors.

Only after I have begun in earnest this reunion process
can I begin the work of becoming the ancestor worthy of

my descendants. Only then will I live into the moral imperative of creating the inclusivity forged in the work of loving and being loved, making myself and others safe, and fostering systemic Belonging as the counteraction to systemic Othering.

What secrets lay behind the myths your family told to make sense of their journey? What are the stories—the facts—they didn't want to know or tell, for example, about your family? Which branches, or buds, on your family tree have been forgotten or discarded?

Opening oneself to such stories might challenge your perceptions of your family's worthiness to belong, but it will release you from the shadowed weight of unsaid, unknown things. Reuniting with the reality of your ancestral journeys—however unpleasant they may feel—will open you to the possibility of seeing that the others' story is, in the end, your story.

CHAPTER 3

Longing for the Elders

What will it take to heal the generational wounds
of unknowing and separation? Reunion and story
sharing . . . We were created for radical connectedness.

—LISA SHARON HARPER, *FORTUNE*

Here's a story that could be a myth. Nevertheless, it's true. Mom and Dad stand before the altar at Holy Cross Church in Flatbush, Brooklyn. Dad, as skinny as a young Frank Sinatra, his thick hair wet and slicked back in a just-satisfactory pompadour, leans slightly forward, while Mom, just over three months pregnant, tries to settle herself, nervous and jittery in her off-white dress, before the priest.

Mom's father, Dominick, is tight-lipped and straight-backed. Mom's mother, Nicoletta, smiles sadly; her body leans crookedly, hinging forward and to the right, the years in a corset taking their toll.

Dad's father, Vito, is a short, squat fireplug of a man, his fedora resting in his lap.

Dad's mother, Maria, is agitated. She paces at the back of the church, angry, hurt, defeated. Her son is the light of her life. No one is good enough for him. His crinkly smile and piercing blue eyes light up whatever room he occupies. He is her treasure. And now he has been ensnared by the wily temptress, my mother, Jean, who lacks class and refinement. The loss of her son brings Maria back to all the losses she has ever experienced, all the way back to the braying donkeys and fig trees of Palo del Colle.

The altar boys flank the priest, who chooses to overlook the off-white of Jean's dress. One boy punctuates the rites with a clanging swing of the censor, while the other reverently clasps his hands, hoping that someone, anyone, will tip them at the end of the wedding.

Maria, still pacing, can't stand it any longer. She screams a deep wail borne in her barren womb: "Puttana!"

"Puttana!" she screams once more in the dialect of Bari, the second syllable drawing out and into a sob so deep that it finds its roots in Palo del Colle. "Puttana!"

"Whore," she calls my mother. "Whore." She hurls the word from the back of the church, cursing the God who's now taking from her the only thing she ever really cared about: her son.

Her son. She wrestles the words over in her mind as the whole assembly turns toward her, waiting for what might come next. Then she explodes: "Cazzate!" "Bullshit!"

Turning to her treasure, her son, she reaches deep within to declare, "And you," she screams, "you're no son of mine!"

The organist stops. The priest presiding over the nuptials goes silent. Jerry and Jean, my parents, standing next to each other, look down at their feet, shame washing over them. Dominick and Nicoletta, standing in the front pew, closest to the altar, shift their weight from foot to foot.

"You're no son of mine! You never were and never will be."

And that's how my father found out he was adopted.

Or that's how my mother would tell the story. Of course, it could be a myth.

THE PRINCES OF PALO DEL COLLE

For me, the story mixes with my own memories and myths. As I became a teenager, I began to let go of the myth of our having belonged to a line of princes. I settled into an uneasily held notion that home, my home, was where that fig tree had first sprouted back in Palo del Colle.

Late at night, we youngest kids in bed, my parents would battle, my mother hurling fragments of that story at my father's heart. His crinkly smile and bright blue eyes dulling under the influence of another Pabst Blue Ribbon.

You're no son of mine.

I slept on the bottom of a bunk bed I shared with my brother Dom; he up top, occasionally lifting a mattress edge, teasing me by pretending to spit on me.

Puttana!

You're no son of mine.

That story remains wrapped in gauzy myth mostly because, my mother's verbal assaults notwithstanding, we never really talked about it. My father died before we ever spoke about it. I never asked him what it meant to find out that his past was a myth. What was it like to discover at twenty-one years old that those to whom you thought you belonged weren't, in fact, your people? Who were you really if not the son of Vito and Maria? Where were your roots if not in Puglia?

I couldn't know the answers to these questions, but I could imagine.

Sometimes, often only with a Pabst Blue Ribbon nearby,

his blue eyes would glisten slightly, and he would speak about Palo del Colle. As best as I know, he never visited there. American-born, he never found his way "home." The closest he came was just after World War II ended. When he was part of the American forces, he'd made his way up through Italy and then, later, to Germany—to Berlin, Munich, and Nuremberg.

He'd speak of the Italy as home to the only people to whom he knew he belonged. And I can imagine him, though, with the wound that comes from wondering, "To whom do I *really* belong?"

REMEMBER YOUR BIRTH

To whom do any of us belong? Of the many wounds of childhood that manifest in the leadership challenges of my clients, the lack of Belonging—and its attendant acceptance, love, and the resulting sense of safety—is the most haunting, the most troubling. The lack of Belonging, especially that which stems from a missing elder, can create an emptiness, a hollowness that swallows up joy and the ability to love another.

I'm reminded of Augustus—Gus, for short. A would-be early-stage investor, a not-quite-yet-successful businessman, Gus persisted in his efforts to come see me. For months, he'd been checking to see if I had time for him. At our first appointment, he sat nearly silent. I sat opposite him and waited.

Months of discussions followed about the investment fund he was trying to create—because of family connections he had access to millions of dollars of capital. Our discussions tended to stay in the head and away from the heart. We spent more time talking about his investment strategy than about why he was sitting on my couch in the first place.

And yet he never failed to show up for his sessions. One day, I steered the conversation to his father. He'd told me that his father had passed away just months before we'd begun meeting.

Gently, I asked where Gus was when his father had passed. He began crying. "I was on an airplane," he said. He'd been in the United States, his father in France. His mother had called because his father had been acting strangely, locking himself in a bedroom all day, for example. In hindsight, they realized he'd been struggling with depression.

Gus was on a flight when his father leaped from a hotel balcony. He'd come to me, I realized, not so much for the practical advice of a former venture capitalist on how to raise and deploy a fund. He'd come to me to remember his father, to find his missing elder. He'd come because the resulting broken heart had robbed him of words and feelings. He felt, he told me, that he needed forgiveness for not being there to stop his father.

"There was nothing you could do," I told him. "Your father's path was his path." I then shared a teaching that my beloved Buddhist teacher, Sharon Salzberg, had taught me, about easing my own hollowed-out heart: "All beings own their own karma," I shared. "Their happiness or unhappiness depends on their actions, not my wishes for them."

He resisted, so profound was his sense of duty to the elder, to the father, that it was nearly impossible for him not to feel responsible for his father's sadness, let alone his own.

I then spoke from someplace deep within me, someplace where my own feelings of being both a son and a father reside. I said, "I forgive you, Gus. I have always loved you and am sorry I left you."

Startled, Gus caught his breath. He remembered all there was to remember about his times with his father—the times they'd shared, the dreams they'd compared, the heartaches that led them to despair.

The words were followed by tears. Over time, our conversations shifted away from sorting through the intricacies of being a successful investor and toward understanding that he'd done nothing wrong. He hadn't caused his father to take his own life by not being a good enough son. He came to understand that his desire to be a good investor was fueled largely by a desire live up to his father, the great business executive. Gus, who'd always defined himself as caught between worlds, always living within the shadow of his great man father, finally came to see that he was good enough just as he was. And more, that his father in all likelihood simply wanted him to live a good life. As we ended our sessions, his true work was done. His reunion with the missing elder completed.

This reunion brings to mind Joy Harjo's poem, an incantation invoking the magic of remembering. In "Remember," she teaches us:

> Remember the sky that you were born under,
> know each of the star's stories.
> Remember the moon, know who she is.
> Remember the sun's birth at dawn, that is the
> strongest point of time. Remember sundown
> and the giving away to night.*

---

* "Remember," from *She Had Some Horses* by Joy Harjo.

Remembering sundown and the giving away to night of the places we called home reunites us with who we truly are. It unites us with those who were born under the same moon, the same stars, and the same sun. It is the reunion from which unity springs.

But how can anyone reunite with anything or anyone from their past when the stories of their births are fabricated memories, myths wrapped in gauze? Hidden truths and protective secrets designed to ward off shame and, ironically, the threat of being cast out, of not Belonging to the family.

How could someone such as my father know the stars that overlooked his birth when his mother wasn't born where he'd always believed? When she wasn't who he thought she was? The only parents he'd ever known turned out to have been myths, screen memories blocking the awareness of his true parents, his true lineage. How could he know to whom he belonged when his body couldn't remember?

"Remember your birth," adds the poet, "how your mother struggled to give you form and breath. You are evidence of her life, and her mother's, and hers." What does it do to a soul who can't remember such things? And, lacking that memory, are you still evidence of your mother's life, and her mother's, and her mother's before her?

How can you remember, how can you belong, when you don't know your father. Or his father. What is the hunger that goes unnourished in the man or woman whose knowledge is screened, whose memories are myths, and whose origins are lost to time and shameful secrets?

Absent ancestors create a hunger for a reunification with the lost elders. Remembering those lost is a core step in the reunion undergirding systemic and sustaining Belonging. Just as Gus was finally able to move on from the loss of his father, we begin the process of reunion by feeling the loss, by speaking to the missing elders, by turning them from ghosts who haunt us into elders who love us. We begin by welcoming the unwelcome, no matter how painful it might be. We welcome back into memory and consciousness those ancestors lost in time, and in doing so, we welcome our elders. And to do that, we begin with the broken hearts.

SENSE AND UNDERSTAND

In her anger and frustration with my father's drinking, my mother would weaponize his lostness, his lack of Belonging. "You drink because you're really German," she would say to a man who witnessed testimony about the Nazis' camps just months after they were liberated.

At other times, she'd say he was *really* Irish. He was born to drink, she'd imply—his love of beer was genetic.

Sometimes he'd fight back, answering her criticisms, her claims of his infidelities. She'd sneer at him, and turning even more cruel, she'd sing him a little Ella Fitzgerald: "Come to me, my melancholy baby," her voice dripping with sarcasm, mocking his obvious depression. "Cuddle up and don't be blue."

In my teens, my anger at his failure to defend himself against my mother's cruelty morphed into disdain. Lying in bed at night, fretting about not getting enough sleep ahead of my five a.m. alarm so that I could make it to school on time, I'd hear him shuffling through the house in his pajamas and black faux-leather slippers.

Each night he'd check the locks on the windows and the door. I hated him for doing that. "What is he so afraid of?" I'd say, my ever-critical teenage voice dripping with contempt at what I took to be his fear. *Cuddle up and don't be blue.*

After his mother died, we moved from my beloved Brooklyn to the house he'd inherited, his childhood home in Ozone Park, Queens. He'd shift about the house, admiring the walls painted a brownish tan that my mother had picked out. He'd sit at the vinyl-covered kitchen table, sighing to my younger brother, John, and me. "It's ours," he'd say through his melancholy smile. "It's ours," he'd repeat, satisfied that, at last, he'd provided a safe refuge for his family.

But I saw none of that at the time. My teen ears heard his sighs as a pathetic confirmation of my mother's withering criticisms. My mother pointed out that, unlike *her* father, the larger-than-life, impossible-to-live-up-to Dominick Guido, with his many Brooklyn buildings, my father hadn't earned our home, hadn't *earned* his place in the world.

I am ashamed now that his satisfied sighs, his subtle ways of telling himself that he had earned his life, made me angry back then. Now, as a father in my own right, I can feel his concern for my safety with each click of the window latch. I can see now that each breathy sigh of "It's ours" wasn't evidence of his failure, but of his deep sense of having finally, ultimately, created a home for himself and those whom he loved.

Each click of the lock must have meant that, despite the withering attacks of his wife, he could finally feel loved, safe, and—because he had earned it—that he belonged.

Of course, I can't know. But as I approach my own elderhood after years of working with my own need to know whether and to whom I belong, I can use curiosity, intuition, and empathic, active imagination to reunite with my father. By imagining what it was like for him to come of age, to enter marriage, parenting, and adulthood, I can find the lost boy and bring him home. And, in doing so, begin to satisfy my hunger to know him, to be his son, and to know the man so that I can be the adult I was born to be.

Perhaps, on those nightly rounds of lock checking, he'd wonder about his birth mother, "Why did she give me up?" Perhaps, as he sat, puzzling out a jigsaw, Pabst Blue Ribbon at hand, half watching *Gunsmoke* on the old black-and-white TV, a whispery voice danced in his head, teasing, haunting him with, "Why did she not want me?"

I imagine him grappling with his own feelings of parenthood. I think of the note he left me in my senior year of high school. It was opening night, and I had a starring role in the play. I was playing Oberon in *A Midsummer Night's Dream*. "Good luck tonight," he wrote in his precise and beautiful handwriting, a penmanship taught by the sturdy strict nuns at St. Mary Gate of Heaven School, just down the street from his home, my home, our home. "Good luck tonight—or as they say, 'Break a leg'—I know you'll be just great—you couldn't be less if you tried." And, with a bit of flourish under the last words that makes me smile every time I read them, "Love, Dad."

Did he know the kind of prideful love he gifted me?

HOW DOES IT SERVE YOU TO *NOT* KNOW?

The Buddhist nun Pema Chödrön, writing in her tiny, powerful book *Welcoming the Unwelcome*, teaches that we should always begin with a broken heart. "Putting so much effort into protecting our hearts from pain hurts us over and over again," she reminds us. "Even when we realize it's unhelpful, this is a hard habit to break." But when we go against the grain of this very human tendency, when we lean into the pain of shame or when we look at the things we don't want to see, know, or remember, when we "arouse the bravery to take a direct look at ourselves and the world," we may then feel the connections between our own pain and the pain of others' experiences. We see that our stories are their stories. In a heart-centered expression of Belonging, in a crucial step in this process of reunion, we see that their stories are our stories. My father's story, in the end, is *my* story.

So I'll blow a kiss to the shame I feel about my teenage anger, let go of the story of my shame, and do justice to his story by inquiring deeply and radically.

What was it that I was so angry about? In some ways, it was about the things I didn't want to know. To know them was to experience them, and experiencing them was unwelcome, unbearable. What didn't I want to know? How did it benefit me, or my family, by not knowing the full story? What did *not knowing* mean?

What does not knowing do for each of us—individually and collectively? For, just as keeping secrets protects aspects of the family myths, just as not knowing what we all know to be true serves a family, so, too, it serves our communities.

What is it that your family or your community prefers to not see? As composer Lin-Manuel Miranda chided in his soundtrack for the movie *Encanto*, "We Don't Talk About Bruno." Each family has a Bruno.

For one, seeing my father's feelings, seeing his having earned it in those satisfied lock-click sighs, meant that I had to acknowledge that his heart may have been broken. Seeing the broken hearts of our parents humanizes them and forces us to give up the anger that allows us to keep their pain from touching our own broken hearts. (Just as not seeing the broken hearts of others keeps their pain at a safe distance from our own.)

Moreover, seeing our parents' broken hearts gives us no choice but to feel our own. Their stories become our stories as our stories become those of our children, our grandchildren, and our great-grandchildren.

More, too, by not seeing his coming of age in his nightly wanderings, his coming home, finally, to a house he could call his own, allowed me to maintain the fabricated myths around the land I wanted to call home: Palo del Colle.

In one small single breath of awareness, in the sighs that filled the house after the daily tumult had finally quieted, was the knowledge that we were never descended from kings and queens. That our lineage of Belonging was complicated and unclear.

My father died just after I'd turned thirty. Despite the love for him that energizes my missing him, I'd been angry at the ways he'd failed me, angry at the ways he failed *us*—my brothers and sisters. Hell, I'd even been angry at his death, at the way he died. I saw his death as a curse. My anger enabled me to avoid the pain. Dying as and when he did deprived me of the ability to ask if he had known how much I was hurt as a boy. Did he know and did he care? And, if he had cared, why didn't he stop it?

His death before I felt my own adulthood settling in made me feel unclaimed and denied. I took some comfort in knowing that he'd known me as a father. My son, Sam, and daughter,

Emma, were each born before he'd passed. He had held each of them. He had loved them both. My heart hurts knowing he never held Michael, the youngest.

In the hole left by the lack of understanding of him as a man, I fabricated stories—of who he was, what he carried in his heart, and to whom he, I, my brothers and my sisters, and, ultimately, my children, belonged.

How did it feel, I wondered, to be the boy with two names? Late at night, as you walked through the house that was finally ours, what did you think of the mother who left you to the nuns and nurses at the foundling hospital? Or of the father who failed to claim you?

Lacking answers, I was left to make my own path toward overcoming the past, creating an adult life, and, ultimately, reaching manhood. Lacking an elder to guide me, I moved to the safety of outward success and into the inner turmoil of my unresolved Belonging. Despite the richness of our outer successes, the inner poverty of our insecure, unanswered longing to belong leaves us bereft and unable to create the conditions for Belonging in our companies and communities.

KNOWING WHAT WE DON'T WANT TO KNOW

Years after Dad had died, my family had gathered for Thanksgiving. The extended table—too big for the kitchen—moved into the living room and into what had been my parents' bedroom. At the time, Mom lived with her cat in the house my father had inherited, the house that was finally his, finally *ours*.

Dinner was nearly over; walnuts, slices of orange, and a little raw fennel had been passed around. The espresso was still on the stove, the deck of cards not yet opened.

Suddenly my brother Vito passed around white envelopes. He'd orchestrated things so that we'd all open the envelopes simultaneously, each coming to know what was inside at the same time.

This was years before I came to own my connection to the observation that James Baldwin had made to the *New York Times*: "When you're writing, you're trying to find out something you don't want to know." Thinking back—feeling once again my reaction and witnessing myself in this moment writing about that which I don't want to know—I feel how much was, and still is, so unwelcome.

Inside those white envelopes were copies of a letter from the adoption agency where my father was first fostered and from which he was later adopted. Vito and my sister Mary had gotten them from New York Foundling Hospital, a name I'd grown up hearing in my mother's weaponized references to his birth.

My father, Jerome Vito Colonna, was, for the first eighteen months of his life, William Michael Heffernan. His first mother wasn't Maria Colonna, wife of Vito Colonna, son of Girolamo Colonna, from Palo del Colle. As she'd revealed, his mother wasn't the woman who screamed at him on his wedding day, but Mary Heffernan, aged twenty-one, when she gave birth.

His father, Timothy O'Connor, was twenty-seven when Mary gave birth. Never marrying Timothy, Mary eventually went home to Thurles, County Tipperary, Ireland. She died in 1988.

Few of these details were in the papers in the envelopes my brother passed around. That day, all I saw was confirmation that Dad was not who I wanted him to be. That day, that information confirmed my grandmother's cruel disowning of my father, confirmed my mother's mocking, heartless, sarcastic attacks. It was confirmation of the unwelcomed.

Years later, my eldest sister, Mary, dove deep into our shared ancestry, trying to find the people to whom he and we Belonged.

"Don't you want to know who she was?" Mary asked one day, speaking of my father's first mother, Mary. No, I answered silently, in my head. I didn't want to know anything about her at all.

I didn't want to know, because knowing would admit the possibility that my father, as well as his descendants, were not wanted. And if he had not been wanted, what of me? To whom did I—my siblings and I—belong?

Better to live with the fabricated myths of lineage than to run the risk of my being unwelcome and Belonging to no one.

The poet Wallace Stevens, in "The Irish Cliffs of Moher," called his ancestors, his father and his father's father, "Shadows like winds." Ghostly shadows who, if they were remembered, might become ancestors and teach the ways of adulthood.

WELCOME THE UNWELCOME

The stories of our parents and their parents and the parents before them are *our* stories. Their pain, their joy—the bones of these dead cry out to remember the sky and the soil that bore witness to their lives and deaths. To find our own sense of Belonging, we must welcome them back into our lives, our memories, and the stories we tell. This reunion with the denied and forgotten parts of ourselves vivifies the process of deeper, more true Belonging.

We remembered them and with that remembering we begin healing the dismembering caused by an unwillingness to know the truth. We no longer need the fabricated myths of long-ago princes, the stories that comforted a scared child by telling him who he was.

I remember the moment when I began to know my father William Michael—dormant within the wind-like shadow of Jerome Vito. That knowledge, that felt sense of who he was, came after I'd entered his house in the company of my son.

My son Michael spent the first part of his senior year studying at Trinity College in Dublin. It was, in many ways, a challenging, lovely, life-affirming rite-of-passage semester abroad. I visited him that December, and we celebrated my fifty-fifth birthday at a restaurant close to the banks of the River Liffey, not far from the Ha'penny Bridge.

Despite the cold and dark, the city was festive. The morning of my birthday, Michael sat for a final exam. We made plans to gather the next day for brunch at a local café at the National Print Museum. The museum was the heart of a complex of buildings celebrating the craft of printers. Stuffed with waffles, eggs, and, for him, bangers, we'd wandered into the museum itself, gawking at mechanical presses and cases of lead type.

The museum's curators had laid out signs and placards that detailed the process that turned lead type into newspapers that informed, books that broke open hearts, and broadsides that fueled revolutions. As we walk the curated path intended to mimic the process of printing, we stopped at a copy of the Irish Declaration of Independence hanging on a stone wall. Michael Collins used the document, with its mismatched and broken type, to rally the faithful in pursuit of the independence and freedom of the Irish people, honoring the dead generations.

The image of the broadside made me realize how little I knew about the Irish Republic's fight for freedom. I wandered through the exhibit, explaining to Michael what I know of the printing process, of the setting of type, of the melting of used type back into its flaming primordial liquified lead.

My son cocked his head somewhat suspiciously, as he always does when I go into far too much detail about something he's surprised I know. "How do you know this, Dad?"

Suddenly I'm ten, and at my father's side as we wander the printing room at Adams-Payne printing, his workplace. I stand close to him as my father's co-worker, our "uncle Frank," swiftly grabs type from the upper and lower cases and pours molten lead to set my name, JEROME COLONNA, in a block. As a byline, there's no need to lock this type into a temporary vise as one might set a page of words bound for a broadside or a newspaper. I treasured that slug of lead, that JEROME COLONNA forever fixed in metal. That byline told me who I was, defining me long before I'd found the ability to open my heart, write from my blood, and discover my own sense of Belonging.

Standing before a linotype machine, my son beside me, I spoke of my father, the boy with two names: William Michael and Jerome Vito. While the figs and olive oil of Palo del Colle flow through the blood of my blood, there are others—ghostly ancestors and lost elders who suffered their own famine— whose blood flows through my veins, as well as through the veins of my son.

In that moment I began to welcome what had been unwelcome. In the mismatched type of that broadside—born of molten lead and the fire that melts metal—is a declaration of more than just the independence of the Irish people. It was a declaration against systemic Othering and for the interdependent Belonging of my ancestors. The point of intersection of these lost elders and my son and me is my father: The boy with two names.

Over the next few days, I floated in a waking dream haunted by the ghosts of my Irish ancestors, I saw their shadows everywhere. "Remember us," they whispered as I walked the streets of Dublin, "look up and remember the sky under which we were born."

ELDER HUNGER

In his book *From Wild Man to Wise Man*, the Franciscan priest, theologian, and teacher Richard Rohr writes that many people experience an immense father hunger, a "huge, aching hole inside that is never really filled." A hole left by the absence of a perfect and unconditional love, a love that is safe and signals acceptance and, ultimately, Belonging. A love that wouldn't be denied when you stood at the altar to marry the mother of your firstborn. A love that would never allow a father to leave unclaimed their firstborn.

The love that protects a child against all that would break them.

Rohr teaches that the lack of such love creates "the single most prevalent absence in the human soul." Prevalent, he notes, and one of the most painful: "The pain is quiet, hidden, denied, and takes many shapes and forms that sons cannot even grasp—or care to grasp."

Sons, yes, but daughters as well. For we cannot be ourselves, none of us can be our own person, until we have been someone else's little child. Loved, made safe, and knowing the sights, smells, and senses of unquestioned Belonging by a parents' never-extinguished regard, we become who we were meant to become.

I'm haunted by that phrase *father hunger*. It's the metaphor of *hunger* that strikes me most deeply, resonantly. I know that hunger. I bear it myself. I have seen it in others.

When I think of those with whom I've worked who've struggled to lead well, to take their seats as the adult leaders they were born to be, I think of the absences in their lives, and I hear the wails of Buddhist hungry ghosts.

According to folklore, hungry ghosts are wraithlike creatures reincarnated after a previous life of harmful desire, greed, anger, and ignorance. They are ghosts—not ancestors—because they remain unsettled, unreconciled, unreunited with the perfect love they sought as children. The resulting hunger is insatiable; there's an aching hole in their hearts created by the absence of love, safety, and Belonging.

Hungry ghosts, then, are bred in the negative space left by absent elders. Absent Belonging, we become ghosts—shadows like wind.

Hungry ghost leaders damage all they lead. As hungry ghosts with power move through the world, they leave unsteady, broken, and groundless hearts in their wake. Just as we cannot be our own person until we become, in Rohr's teaching, someone else's little child, leaders who hunger for elders can never create systems of Belonging until they know to whom, and to where, they belong. Until, that is, they remember the skies of their birth and that of their ancestors. Until they hear the voices of their ancestor elders.

Those who hold power, who have been reborn as elder-hungry ghosts, cannot create systemic Belonging until and unless they are willing to reunite with their past and the dismembered and unremembered parts of themselves and their lineage. The wombs of their birth were empty of love, safety, and Belonging.

My father was born into such an empty womb. He died unclaimed by one elder, his father; abandoned by another, his mother; and disowned by a third, his wife.

To whom do people like him look to know what it means to be a man, a woman, a parent, an adult? Who teaches those of us born into such negative spaces what it means to feel included, to feel safe in the loving arms of Belonging? Who teaches us how to create inclusivity, the felt sense of love, safety, and, most importantly, Belonging for others.

Worse still, when the negative spaces are shielded from knowledge by a lineage that includes dismembering of the truth, the secret keeping of not revealing the truth of a birth until adulthood, until a wedding day, pushing away the unwelcome and the fear of reopening old wounds that keeps people like me from writing about the things we don't want to know, we unconsciously create more negative space. Not to know such things blocks healing and leaves raw and untended the wounds of absent parents, ghostly elders.

FINDING THE WORDS: PETER'S STORY

"Tell me about Dad," I say, and my friend Peter smiles.

Peter has been to many of our boot camps, our leadership retreats. Over the past seven years, we've had many conversations about life and leadership. He smiles because he knows, or thinks he knows, where I'm going with my question.

Over the years, across our many walks and talks, I could never be entirely sure of what it was that Peter was looking for. Sometimes he'd ask simple, seemingly pragmatic questions, like "How should I think about firing this employee?"

More often, though, the topics would wander into deeper existential areas.

"Jerry," he said haltingly, hesitantly, with a hint of an accent, "I can't put it into words but somehow I'm not getting what it is I'm looking for."

One time he shared that his life trajectory had changed because he'd seen a video of a talk I'd given. With that, he signed up for his first boot camp. Another time he shared that, after watching me work with a fellow camper, he'd lain in bed that night and said to himself, "That's what I want to do with my life."

Eventually he'd turned over control of the company he founded and trained to be a coach. Now, years later, we'd reconnected.

"I can't put it into words," he said, using his familiar phrase, "something's just not right."

Pausing in silence, I stared into his eyes and focused my inner eye even further inward. I looked to see what it was I was feeling in that moment so that I could understand even better what it was that *he* was feeling, what *he* was seeking.

And my father's searching, terrified blue eyes came into view. I saw my own dying father. I heard his death-rattled breaths.

"Tell me about Dad," I said.

Tell me the story, I thought, that is at the root of your searching. Tell me of the elder you're searching for. Tell me to whom you're longing to belong.

"Dad was a middle manager," he said. "He was a middle manager who'd made it through."

"Made it through what?" I asked.

"The shit show that was the fall of the Soviet Union," he explained, as if it were obvious. Peter explained that his father had been born in 1946.

"What was it like in 1946?" I asked, very much aware of history but wanting to know his family's experience.

"I suppose there was a celebration at the end of the war . . . but we didn't really talk about it. He didn't talk about it."

"With more than twenty million killed during the World War II," I pointed out, "I imagine every family suffered the loss of a loved one." And then he told me the story that could be a myth.

His father's mother had had two girls during the war. German fighter jets were strafing their town, and his grandmother carried her two toddler girls to the railroad tracks, looking to get out of the town before it was destroyed.

At the tracks, the train was already moving. Grandma had to get on the train, but her arms were laden with her two children. She had no free hand to pull herself and her children onto the train. Looking around quickly, trying to decide what to do, she put one of her daughters down on the ground and lifted herself and her other daughter onto the moving train. Speeding up, the train took her and her daughter away to safety. The other daughter stood beside the tracks, watching the train disappear.

Later, after the war, his grandmother gave birth to her son, Peter's father.

"What did your dad say about his sister, your aunt, left by the side of the tracks?"

"Nothing. We never talked about it. The story was just told as were all the stories of the war. It was just there." There but unwelcome.

"Tell me about Dad," I repeated.

"He was just . . . I don't know . . . there. Like the stories."

There but not there, I felt him say. Absent father breeding a hungry ghost, longing to belong. A generation of elders turned into unsettled ghosts.

Peter stares absently into the distance. Turning back to me, his eyes wet, "I think I know what's missing. I think I'm looking for someone to look up to."

Nodding, I ask, "What does it feel like to not have someone to look up to?"

"Anxious, uncertain," says Peter. "I'm on my own."

I recall the words of Richard Rohr: "If manhood itself does not like me, then I'm forever insecure."

SOMEONE TO LOOK UP TO: PATRICK'S STORY

"What about heroes?" he asked after raising a hand and interrupting the talk I was giving. I was confused. The talk, built around themes from my first book, an exploration of how better humans make better leaders, has a rhythm and cadence to it, and his question surprised me. Do enough talks, do them well, and you develop a sense of when and how people will react. This wasn't the moment I expected a question. And this wasn't a question I'd ever heard before.

"What about heroes?" he asked again.

Wrapped up in my own thoughts, projecting my own feelings into the moment, I assumed he was talking about his father.

"Tell me about Dad," I asked.

"There's nothing to say about him," he spat out. "He was gone before I even knew who he was."

As the senior leader in the room, the person with the power to convene us all, his power had silenced the room. The audience—a mix of his staff, colleagues—went still and quieted.

I then noticed his hair, disheveled, tussled, mussed up. Earlier it had been neatly combed, well styled. I hadn't noticed that he'd been rubbing his head, like a little boy, while I'd spoken about the effects of our childhood on how we are as leaders, as adults.

In the curious space between two humans circling each other and moving toward more intimacy, I was projecting my own experience. I had wanted his question to be about his father.

He continued. "What happens," he asked through sobs, "when you no longer have a hero to look up to?"

"Who's gone?" I asked, finally grokking a bit better where he was headed.

"I'm sorry," he sobbed. "I'm so sorry to have lost it. I'm so sorry." He was apologizing for crying.

I walked over to him, took a knee in front of him, leaned in so no one else could hear, so he could feel a little safer. I repeated, "Who's gone?"

The tightly managed defense melted away: "My mother."

The facade cracked and the dam burst. All that was held back, keeping the little boy whose father left him and his heroic mother safe, flooded the room.

"Mom just died. She was my hero. I don't know who to look up to anymore."

There it is: the yearning for the elder, the longing to belong.

Who do I look up to now? This is the hunger that Peter had expressed and that Patrick was expressing now—the yearning for someone to teach us to be the adult version of ourselves. But this hungry ghost, born in the negative space left by an absent father, was bereft. His firm, it turns out, was drifting because the hungry ghost leader had himself assumed the role of the heroic leader, modeling himself on the only functional and available adult he knew—his mother. In her absence, the powerful, ever-optimistic leader was lost.

On a knee, whispering closely, and, as I had done for the young woman whose ancestors had endured bondage, the middle passage, and subjugation, I called his ancestors into the room.

"What is she telling you right now?" I whispered to him, knowing that his mother, the woman who, alone, had managed the burden of raising this boy into this man, was still in him.

"She's saying, 'You can do it.' She's saying, just as she used to say it to me when I was struggling to read, struggling to do math, struggling all the time. 'You can do it.'"

I see the little child looking to the parent for the reassurance that the world is safe, that they are loved, and that they belong. I see the elder, his elder, looking down, encouraging him to press on.

I think of my daughter, Emma, looking over her shoulder

as she turned to run and play with her friends at the playground. "Can I really climb the monkey bars, Daddy?"

"You can do it." I'd willed the spirit of those words into her six-year-old body at Pine Street playground.

"Can I really leave home and take up a life at college?" my daughter asks with her eyes as I fold up the last of the cardboard boxes containing so much of her life and fastened the 3M Command strips so she'll always have a place to hang her keys.

"You can do it," I say into the warm, wet embrace of a hug that I want to go on forever.

"You're my hero," she whispers silently, her head buried into the crook of my neck, as she did when she was weeks old and would wake in the night, cold, wet, hungry, worried that she was alone.

"You can do it," I answer back.

Elder hunger, the hunger for the invitation into adulthood that is our birthright, manifests differently for each of us.

The poet Richard Shelton, in "Letter to a Dead Father," wrote that "fathers who cannot love their sons have sons who cannot love." It was not the father's fault, adds the poet, nor the son's. But the result is the same: the boy who hungers for the elder's love must recover without it. "Now I no longer need anything." Yet in that not-needing are the unquenchable needs of the hungry ghost.

"IT'S NOT ABOUT ME": ANDY'S STORY

"I want you to write on your mirror in dry-erase ink 'It's not about me,'" I tell my client Andy. "I want you to see that every morning when you shave or brush your teeth."

Andy's mother haunts him daily. His father, absent in spirit, would sit silently as his mother would pass along her own anxieties with a relentless push for improvement. Andy, in turn, irritates his colleagues; nothing they do is ever good enough. As it was for him as a boy, so it is for him as a man, as a leader, as the one with the most power.

"Tell me about Grandpa," I asked one day, following my intuition.

"There's not much to say. He died in the famine after World War II."

"How old was your mother?" I ask.

"I don't know . . . I guess she was about ten."

"When you were a boy," I continue, following the seam, "how safe was Mom?"

"Oh my God! She was never safe. She catastrophized everything. If I were to go for a walk, she'd worry about my being run down by a car. If I were to play with my friends, she'd worry that they would hurt me.

"She was never safe," he repeats. "She was always so insecure."

Her forever-insecurity inhibiting her ability to be his elder.

He pauses, looks back at me with new eyes. "Is this why I see everything as a threat? Is this why every threat is to me personally?"

I answer, smiling, "It's not about you, Andy.

"Now, the other thing I'd like you to write on your mirror: 'I'm safe.'"

CHASING DAD, CHASING MONEY: COLIN'S STORY

Larry was eight when he watched his father beat his mother and walk away and out of their lives forever. His forever-insecurity led him to create a company where conflict was to be avoided at all costs.

When the parents of another client, Colin, were divorcing, his father had a choice: revoke the trust he'd set up for his sons and take back the money he'd earmarked for their future (and their children's futures) or split custody with Colin's mother. His father chose the money.

It wasn't clear when we first started working together that Colin was a hungry ghost. He said he'd come to coaching to define a new career. His persistent, nearly paranoid fear and anxiety then were obstacles from the start. He saw threats everywhere. Forever insecure.

A boy with no elders with whom he could talk, Colin was searching for a missing elder, and I became a surrogate father.

Slowly, the true consequences of his father hunger revealed themselves. First, it was an insatiable need to be told he was loved. Then it was the inability to soothe himself to the point of safety; his fears led him to see threats around every corner.

No matter the success, no matter how close he came to the things he said he wanted—a rewarding career, a caring family, partnerships with co-founders that felt more like siblings than co-workers—the more frightened he became.

But in the end, our coaching did little to mitigate the other defenses that had formed when his father's theft and abandonment had threatened and shattered the boy.

After the shattering, the boy put back together the leftover fragments as best as he could. He was a success in school. He got married. Became a father.

But the hungry ghost lived on. To be safe, this shattered, still-fragile adult put those fragments into compartments. Compartmentalization kept friends apart from family. In the business he'd co-founded, it kept colleagues from knowing the facts—of the business, of each other's experiences, of what Colin believed, of his truth.

The shattered, compartmentalized, mythical powerful leader became central to every drama in the company's short history. This heroic story made him safe since no one could leave him. Moreover, no one could take away this safety if he was the only one who knew all the secrets. The result was a tangled ball of distrust between and among all employees. In the end, echoing his father's long-ago choice, Colin chose money over the relationships. He chose the safety of money, the pursuit of financial safety over belonging and love.

Fortunately for his colleagues and co-founders, Colin chose to leave. The company began to thrive, and he found the ultimate safety in being a solo entrepreneur.

COME ON HOME

One night, while working through this chapter, I dreamed of my father.

In the dream, I'm at my old family home on Litchfield Road, in Port Washington, New York. There's a ladder against the side of the house. I look up and see a man at the top of the ladder working on the roof. It's my father, and I'm surprised because I never saw him as a handyman. He looks down at me and asks for my help. Will I help him with some of the shingles?

As we work to fix the roof, my father tells me about a beautiful, hidden creek that runs through the property. It's autumn, and the ground's covered with golden leaves. They cover and float on top of the creek. I'm excited because I know about the creek. "I know!" I say excitedly, like a little kid. And I feel so connected to him. There's a secret that we share.

In the house, my father had gathered and piled up many of my things. He wants me to go through the pile before he gets rid of it. He is clearing the house, making room for the new folks who will soon occupy it. I go through the things, and pull out a few items. I don't need these items—I want them. "I have room for these," I say. "I have room for all of it."

I then whisper to him, letting him in on my secret: "I'm not going to sell the house. I will keep it forever." He smiles. I've made him happy.

The dream was a kind of reconciliation with my father as well as the emerging elder in me. In the dream, I got to work on a house with my father. But in the dream, I also committed to making and keeping a forever home.

And it was my father, my missing elder, who was being handy. He was helping me make a home, a true home. For that house was where my youngest son, Michael, came home after being born.

What's more, my father was able to see my first true home. I have video of him at my daughter's first birthday. In it, he watches his granddaughter play with her gifts, his hand resting on the handle of the cart used to tow around the canister of oxygen that kept him alive. Tubes snaking around his head and into his nostrils. He would die of pneumonia weeks later.

I am different now than I was when I denied him at his deathbed. Back then, I was angry with him for not protecting me.

I am no longer angry. Now I'm sorry. I am so sorry I hurt him.

"He's changed," I tell my therapist, speaking of my father. But, of course, it's not he who's changed.

In the years since he died, I've grown up; I've become the man I've wanted to be. And he's changed as a result. He's wiser now. As I move into my own elderhood, I see his.

I am reconciled not with the man I was so angry with. And not with the man whom I wanted him to be. But by reconciling with the man he was, the man he always was, he could become the elder, the father with whom I could play catch, fix gutters, and put roofs over the heads of my children, his descendants.

It was my father who delivered me. On the day of my birth, my mother went into labor suddenly, unexpectedly. Labor progressed quickly, and while my older siblings stood apart, my father delivered me from my mother. The story, the myth of my birth, is that as I came forth, my father noted that "this one has broad shoulders." Those broad shoulders, upon which so many would come to rest, were my father's blessing, even if it at times they felt like a curse.

Parent and child, together we belong to those laboring princes and princesses, those brave souls who left all, who broke their hearts and their backs and built hearths and homes. As much as we belong to anything, we belong to them.

What are the stories of your own hunger? Whose voice, smell, or embrace does your heart yearn for? Where are the elders in your own life and what would they say to you if you welcomed them home?

CHAPTER 4

A Room Called Remember

We know ourselves through the art and act of
remembering. Memories offer us a world where there
is no death, where we are sustained by rituals of regard
and recollection . . . I pay tribute to the past as a
resource that can serve as a foundation for us to revision
and renew our commitment to the present, to making
a world where all people can live fully and well; where
everyone can belong.

—BELL HOOKS, *BELONGING: A CULTURE OF PLACE*

Dreams reinforce the importance of visiting the psychic basements where memories are stored, and they often tell us how to fix that which has been broken. Visiting such basements, these rooms called Remember, is a necessary step in the reunion process. For it is through visiting rooms of our mind that we remember our lives. "The name of the room is Remember—the room where with patience, with charity, with quietness of heart," noted theologian Frederick Buechner— "We remember consciously to remember the lives we have lived." Conscious re-membering resurrects our wholeness from the dismembering wounds, especially those hidden by shame. Reunion with memories, like writing about the things that we do not want to know and speaking the unsaid things, offers us a way to overcome the primal separation of our lives. We *re-member*, and therefore reunite, with the entirety of ourselves, including those parts unknown and unwelcomed.

This reunion, as bell hooks notes, becomes the foundation of revision and renewal wherein we are sustained by "rituals of regard and recollection." In this way, all may live fully and well, and all may belong.

By bravely entering such rooms, by exploring the basements of our psychic homes, by sorting the toys and bearing the attendant flooding memories, we reunite with the abandoned, unclaimed, unwelcomed parts of ourselves. By reclaiming what was unwelcomed, we further our own Belonging and, thereby, create the conditions that might ripen into systemic Belonging for others.

The door to that room, though, should be marked with a warning. Dante told us that those who hope to pass through the gates of hell should abandon all hope. But the rooms of remembering are not hell. The only hope that needs to be abandoned when you commit to remember is the hope and expectation of peaceful oblivion that comes from not remembering. For remembering and, as the Buddhist nun Pema Chödrön teaches, welcoming the unwelcome all too often break our hearts.

DISMAYED BY OURSELVES

The remembrance of such past things often means encountering and embracing the pain that initiated the dismemberment. We dismember ourselves as an adaptation to the pain and wounds of our childhood. We forget so that we may feel safe.

In his essay "Encountering the Stranger," Parker Palmer

notes that we need to reconnect with the othered parts of ourselves; it is the only ground from which we can begin to address systemic Othering of others.

"How can I affirm another's identity when I deny my own?" he writes. "When we can't embrace the stranger within, or even admit to it, we can't possibly embrace the stranger without." To be clear, we will never create a sense of safety and Belonging for others until we develop a sense of safety and Belonging in ourselves, *with* ourselves. Belonging to ourselves like this means reconciling with our ancestors and rescuing the stories that have been buried by shame.

We must allow ourselves, he continues, "to be dismayed by ourselves" and to be honest about our contradictions, our dismembered souls, the places of inner and outer misalignment.

I'll add to Parker's assertion by noting that we fear remembering because we fear encountering the stranger within; the one who embodies the unwelcome parts of ourselves. Facing the stories, wishes, dreams, and beliefs that are the fabric of our memories may demand a radical realignment and reexamination of all that we believe to be true.

We fear the room called Remember because we fear the truth of our history, our being, and our Belonging. We fear the contradictory discoveries that may hide in our memories. To stay safe, we forget and, in doing so, we dismember ourselves from the sources of our Belonging.

OTHERING OUR OWN SELVES

We come by this pattern honestly. Indeed, this pattern is often one of the beliefs we inherit from our ancestors, especially those who themselves were dismembered from their past—

either through effect of gauzy, family creation myths, the willful disregard of truths, or enforced diaspora.

Think of the stories, people, and experiences your family simply choose not to speak about. I have a client, Isaac, who, despite the family myth that they speak about all things, doesn't really know why his great-grandfather fell out of the family tree. "I always suspected something bad had happened to him," he told me one day while we sat under the cottonwood. "But my father just wouldn't talk about it."

Wouldn't talk about it. Wouldn't even allow an exploration of the past, actively denying an understanding of the reality of an ancestor. And then, one day, Isaac found a newspaper clipping. His father's grandfather had hanged himself in the Great Depression.

When confronted with the evidence, Isaac's father denied the facts: "No, no, no . . . that's not right. He was just sick. He just died." The "He just died" myth stands in the way of the unclaimed and denied reality, and the great-grandfather remains a ghost instead of a remembered ancestor, a welcomed elder. The true history of the long-dead ancestor, forgotten and shunted aside along with their original surname, was left in the processing halls of Ellis Island.

Like me, Isaac has had a yearslong struggle with depression. As I did for so many years, he struggled with self-loathing no matter his outward success. Worse, Isaac's father often shamed him for acknowledging his struggles.

And this habitual hiding of the facts threads its way through the family, allowing its destructive power to grow. It grows despite and because it was unacknowledged. The unclaimed sadness of the ancestor resiliently finding expression in the life and curiosity of a newspaper clipping.

Families who refuse to remember often live in wordless prisons whose bars are reinforced by unclaimed feelings.

Such is the power of shame. Even its *potential* can prevent a man from acknowledging his grandfather's pain—a pain so deep that he might have taken his life to escape it. A pain so pervasive as to be a part of a family's lineage, an inheritance as sure as the names we pass from one generation to another. Such is the reason why, perhaps, my client still wonders if his father loves him. "Is he ashamed of my depression," Isaac ponders, "and, if so, how does he feel about the whole of me?" Isaac wonders, if you will, about the solidity of his Belonging.

Families wall off the truth, causing children to become disconnected from essential parts of themselves (often leading to their own depressing lack of Belonging).

For this is how our families survive. We forget things, mask them over with tales that reinforce beliefs designed to keep us safe and repeat patterns of Othering in a perverse pursuit of permanent unshakable Belonging. After all, we have survived by shaking off the chalk marks that the guardians at the gates at Ellis and Angel Islands marked on our jacket lapels to signify our entrance into this other land. We survived by keeping quiet, by trying to belong, to move toward safety even as others were left behind. Survival depended on forgetting, on telling only one side of the story.

WHAT IS IT YOU DON'T WANT TO KNOW?

James Baldwin's breathtaking challenge, to write about the things that we don't *want* to know, requires that we first ask ourselves what it was that our families didn't want to know.

What is it that you yourself don't want to know, and more,

what don't you want to remember? About yourself, about your families, your ancestors, your past?

When we confront such questions, the resulting remembrance of the dismembered thing's past reunites and reassembles in a way that allows us to then open to the other.

Growing up with unsaid things leaves one choking on words that need to be said and feelings that need to be shared. Unsaid things also choke the pathways of connection—to us, yes, but, most heartbreakingly, to others. They block us from hearing what others, especially those who live in the shadows and on the margins of our dominant cultures, desperately need us to hear.

These unsaid, unnamed things root into the soil of our lives, our organizations, and our societies, the rot climbing slowly upward through the plant of our communities and families until, and at last, they can no longer be endured. Violence, both inward and outward, bursts through the silence, revealing deep heartache and crushed souls. Souls crushed by such deeply rooted unsaid, unnamed truths can never feel loved, safe, or that they belong.

Even with the power that may come from the privilege afforded by gender or race, such crushed souls struggle to create love, safety, and Belonging for others.

Such is the power of the unsaid.

But fortunately, there is a way. A reunion process that includes talking about the unsaid is freeing. It makes visible the invisible and frees the words that too often choke, holding back the felt sense of what is right and true. Imagine our communities peopled by those who hold power being dedicated to freeing words and feelings and focused on what is right and true.

As happened for those who read my stories in *Reboot*, my story becomes their story. And, more importantly, their stories—especially the stories of those marginalized by systemic Othering—become our stories. That is a reunion of all beings. It is the ground of what the Buddha taught is our interbeing. Interbeing is the field that nourishes and satisfies hungry ghosts and where systemic Belonging may flourish.

Think of it as discovering and uncovering our origin stories and juxtaposing those against the creation myths our families used to ward off shame and guard their precious belongings and sense of Belonging. Essential to the work I do in helping folks take their seat as openhearted warrior leaders is an exploration of these origin stories.

Yes, I will say, "Tell me about Dad," but I will also ask about Mom, and grandparents and their stories. It helps to understand all the ancestors, all the elders.

Unlike what many of us have been taught to fear, such remembrance of both myth and story doesn't have to trap us in the past. Remembering the grandfather who lost his battle to depression doesn't condemn a man to be haunted by ghosts but frees a dead soul. It is how the dead are made whole again. Remembering our true origin stories, out loud or in the solitude of journaling, can give us the momentum to move toward a healing and healed future.

"I use my journal," wrote memoirist Louise DeSalvo in her moving memoir, *Vertigo*, "as a way of making things better, of fixing things, and of healing myself, and as a way of taking a 'fix' on my life. Of seeing where I am, and plotting a course for the future."

I've taken many a fix on my own life. I've spent many predawn hours remembering not only the far distant past of my childhood but also the near distance of the previous day's heartbreak. In those predawn hours, often with a cup of hot coffee, a heavy pen that fits snugly in my large hands, and the blank page of a journal, I've not only fixed things but encountered the estranged parts of my own character, letting go of the incessant command to ruminate on my own failings.

The fix on my future self always required going beyond the good/bad splitting of my own self. It requires, to paraphrase Parker Palmer, seeing myself as "both/and" and not "either/or." Getting a fix on *your* life requires that you move beyond seeing yourself in pieces labeled "good" or "bad." Following that re-membering, you're able to move beyond seeing others as "good" or "bad." Or, possibly, even as "other."

Indeed, this transformation of consciousness beyond dismemberment and separation, especially by those of us who hold power in a racialized, Othering world, demands that we explore the rooms of memories and surface and hold the contradictions that define our character, our being, as well as that of our ancestors.

I am a descendant of those who were Othered, for example, but I am also a descendant of those who did not use their power and privilege to address the lack of Belonging others encountered, despite the stories of others being so akin to their own stories. Despite their stories being our stories.

How did your ancestors respond to the Othering they may have encountered? How might their response have benefited you? How might it continue to benefit you to this day? The challenges they experienced paradoxically becoming the source material for the privilege of their descendants' lives.

Such complexity, says Palmer, requires us to withstand and not resolve into simple structures the paradox of our stories of Belonging. "When we hold our contradictions as paradoxes in which two poles complete rather than compete with each other," he writes, the resulting "tension can pull us open to a more capacious way of receiving ourselves and our world."

The world of those safe in their Belonging, of course, as well as the worlds of the Othered.

The embracing of the paradoxical contradictions of our past and character, like the welcoming of the unwelcome, begins with being with our broken hearts, allowing the workmen to fix what is broken while we reacquaint ourselves with the memory-flooding toys of our past.

The rooms called Remember are often located in the basements of our psychic homes, next to boilers in need of repair. Time and again, the metaphoric art of the collective unconscious teaches us that the treasures we seek are in the back of the cave, the dark of the subterranean, the basements of our souls' homes.

THE SHAWL OF BELONGING

Over the last year, during the latter stages of the COVID pandemic, bingeing on TV shows replaced the perpetual motion of business and personal travel that had marked so much of my adult life. As for so many, the speediness of life slowed. Unwittingly, so slowly as for me to barely notice, I settled into a life that seemed more like my father's than I'd ever experienced before.

As a boy, my evenings were marked by Dad watching episodes of *Gunsmoke*. For me, it was the BBC's *Call the Midwife*.

I found soothing the repetitive nature of the simple plot-lines, most involving a dramatic, wondrous home birth. The images of the streets of East London's Poplar District in the 1950s and 1960s comforted me. The weathered brick of Non-natus House, the prams parked outside homes with babies sleeping in the fresh air, the streets filled with folks who knew your family, knew your stories, and who thought nothing of telling you, a kid, when you'd done something wrong—all of it felt familiar. Their stories were my stories.

The wimpled nuns and lay midwives serving the poor re-minded me of my hometown streets of Flatbush, Brooklyn. The cul-de-sac outside the nuns' Nonnatus House brought me back to the corner of Newkirk and Nostrand Avenues, where a statue of the crucified Christ stood guard over a subway entrance. Seeing it when we'd returned home from a trip to Abraham & Straus, to see the department store Santa, was the first sign that I was home.

"I love that show," my sister Nicki said to me one morning. "I used to watch it every Sunday night."

We laughed, considering how much it reminded us of home. Even the rats and cockroaches of the appallingly poor houses of Poplar were not so shocking and, oddly, familiar. Our basement could have such visitors, despite the traps set by my grandfather and the Johnston's No Roach my mother would apply to the crevices and dark places of our ground-floor apartment.

"I was watching an episode the other night," I told Nicki, "and I thought of Mrs. Pennington, your teacher. I had such warm feelings. It was odd because I never really knew her."

Nicki quieted, and through the phone I could feel her

settling into her own memories. "She was so sweet," Nicki sighed. "She was so good to me. I loved her."

"I have this vague memory of her giving me a blanket when I was born," I noted. "Obviously it was a story I was told . . . but did Mrs. Pennington give me a blanket?"

"It was a shawl," she corrected. "A white shawl. It was for your christening." She paused, heading back into the room called Remember and feeling her way back in time. "I suppose she knew what was going on at home."

What was going on at home was that, shortly after I was born, Mom went away. Again. As had happened after my sister Annie's birth, Mom had had a breakdown.

"Was it within hours?" I asked my sister. "Was it within days?" I asked before she could respond. "Or weeks?" When had I been separated from Mom? When did Mom leave?

"I don't remember," said Nicki. My sister was nine when Mom went away after my birth. She went to the mental hospital, Pilgrim State.

"I stayed with Cousin Nick and his wife, Carole," Nicki continued. Mrs. Pennington, her fourth-grade teacher and "a wonderful woman," picked her up each day and drove her to St. Jerome School, down the street from the giant statue of the crucified Christ, so she wouldn't miss class.

The christening shawl was for the ritual in which not only was I claimed by God as his child but I was also given my father's name, tying me to the lineage of the poor princes of Palo del Colle. I was claimed by the father into whose hands I was delivered from my mother.

With me, Mom went into labor unexpectedly. It could have been because she'd previously given birth to five kids. Or it could have been because her sense of impending labor was dulled by the primitive anti-psychotic medications she was taking. Whatever the cause, there was no time to get to the hospital. Into the bathroom with you, I imagine my father telling her. Onto the toilet with you, I hear him saying. That move would give rise to the cruel stories of my having been first baptized with toilet water.

It also gave rise to my father's blessing that sometimes, oftentimes, felt like a curse.

I have only borrowed memories of Mrs. Pennington and the shawl. I don't know why, perhaps because of photos my sister has shared. In my mind I know what Mrs. Pennington looks like, even though she was never my teacher. When I close my eyes, I travel across space and time, and seem to remember what the shawl felt like against my bare skin and soon-to-be anointed forehead: scratchy, warm, comforting.

Such memories, borrowed as they are from Nicki, tie us together. Her story becoming part of our story, our story joining my story, and so her story becoming my story. And my story, in turn, becoming hers.

Wrapped in and comforted by a shawl of Belonging, Mrs. Pennington was tied to Nicki as Nicki is tied to me. So strong are those ties that even now, more than fifty years later, the borrowed memories enable me to know that while Mom may have left me, my sisters—Nicki, Mary, Annie—never did. I belonged to them. I still do.

There's a tattered black-and-white photo of me, dressed in a white hat, in a carriage. From the photo, I borrow memories of being held, loved, and made safe by Nicki and Mary and Annie—each of whom was far too young to take on the duties of parenting their younger brothers, Dom and John and me. (Vito, the oldest, was already studying at the seminary, to which he had escaped from the chaos that was our home.) Such memories are borrowed, of course, because a months-old child can't remember the sounds of his sisters' black-and-white saddle shoes as they strike the pavement outside 377 East Twenty-Sixth Street, Flatbush, Brooklyn. Shoes that completed the uniform that defined a child as part of the community that was St. Jerome School.

I have my own memories, of course. These include John the grocer, who let us run up a tab at his shop on the corner of Rogers Avenue and Avenue D—tick marks and pencil scribbles in a tattered black-and-white composition book, following the pencil scratching on a brown paper sack where John would tally our purchases of milk, cheese, and Wonder bread. I know now that tab was often not fully paid.

I have memories of the yearly bazaar at St. Jerome, legalized gambling, and cotton candy. I remember the doughnut shop across the street from the church, where the whole community seemed to head after mass, breaking the communion fast with a glazed chocolate or a French cruller.

The doughnut shop was next to L.O. Grand, the discount department store where Mom would take us for everything from thread to the very occasional treat of a Matchbox car. I remember one time Mom splurging and spending far more than we could afford for a new pair of sneakers for me. They were purple: purple canvas uppers and purple rubber bottoms. From the window, they looked wondrous. After my begging and pleading, and after Mom checked to see if I really, really wanted them, she turned over the money to the man behind the counter.

I remember stepping out into the sunshine in those bright, shockingly purple sneakers and realizing that my feet looked enormous in them. That I had made a mistake. That they were terrible and that I would be made fun of by the kids on East Twenty-Sixth Street.

I said nothing, though. I knew then that we couldn't afford to replace them with another pair. We couldn't waste the money. And so I wore those ugly sneakers until, like every other pair of shoes any of us ever had, they fell off my feet.

Years later, when I was a father myself, I took my daughter, Emma, shopping. Like me, she was transfixed by a particular pair. Like me, her heart sang as her parent said yes to the dreamed-of pair. And, like me, she regretted the purchase the minute we stepped out of the store.

But unlike me, she spoke up. She told me she had changed her mind. Her father heard her, and marched back in to buy a second pair, proving once again that he was no longer the boy in Brooklyn stuck in purple sneakers that he couldn't stand and couldn't leave behind.

"He's gonna carry a lot," said my father at my birth. Not the weight carried by Grandpa Guido—blocks of ice up the stoops of Flatbush (securing payment, Democratic votes, and his family's future along his route). Not the weight of laboring as my ancestor carried, but the weight of secrets within a troubled family who struggled to pay a grocer's tab and a persistent sense of love, safety, and Belonging in the hearts of the kids seated around that table.

I still carry those troubles.

Indeed, even now they give rise to words that need to be spoken, to say things that needed to be said, to see the invisible and unseen, to name what is right and true even when, even if, it breaks me.

"I AM WHAT I CHOOSE TO BECOME."

"I am not what has happened to me," the psychologist Carl Jung wrote. "I am what I choose to become."

That guidance has been my mantra for decades. It's often rescued me from the depths of rumination, story making that compounded my fears while striving to make me feel safe.

My father's dreamy, gauzy disappearances into cans of Pabst Blue Ribbon and episodes of *Gunsmoke*, and his gut-wrenching, heart-rending memories of his non-Belonging left me hungering for a man to tell me what it was to be a man. Despite her undeniable physical presence, with all her terrifying expressions of mental illness, Mom's disappearances—into her dismembered mind or the hospitals that were supposed to heal her—I felt motherless.

I hungered for ancestors and elders to show me the way and to answer my own longing to belong. Dislocation, fragmentation, and groundlessness filled the motherless-ness, father-hungry hole in my heart. It turned me into a hungry ghost.

Ill and absent mothers, fathers whose love was inaccessible, unsaid, and, therefore, unfelt, feed the unsaid things that give rise to the unbidden actions that undermine love, safety, and, most of all, Belonging.

Colin tried to fill the gap in his heart with money, squeezing every dime and breaking the only true things that matter: The love of friends and family. Convincing himself that adoration was love, he never really understood that adoration is merely a facsimile of love.

Gus felt his father's absence long before the leap from the balcony, his father's suicide only confirming Gus's elder-less wanderings into adulthood.

I see now that what happened to me . . . happened. But it does not determine what I choose to be, what I choose to dedicate my life to. Remembering allows me to make the unconscious conscious, thereby putting me back in charge of my own life.

Remembering the ways in which my own sense of Belonging was challenged allows me to determine, with adult power, the Belonging I may create for others.

"Memories," noted poet bell hooks, "offer us a world where there is no death." No death, perhaps, but certainly no bittersweet passage of time.

It was no coincidence that, as I entered the room called Remember, I came away with the story of Mrs. Pennington's shawl. The shawl is proof, if you will, that my brothers and sisters were not forgotten and entirely abandoned to the effects of our parents' pain. Remembering that shawl, a blanket of belonging, if you will, transforms the loss of attachment into an embrace of connection that, even today, connects my sister and me in the knowledge that, despite what we had come through, we were not bad, considering all.

I have this image of time-traveling all the way back to a dark, wintry night in Brooklyn and wrapping my seven-year-old self in Mrs. Pennington's shawl—which would warm his freezing body—and walking him into the embrace of loving sisters who did their best to care; reunited under the shawl, remembering all that needs to be remembered so that the unsaid things no longer lead to unbidden actions.

What didn't I want to know? What didn't I want to find out? What were the secret unsaid things not only in my family but within my own heart? What secrets lay in my own multichambered, compartmentalized, protected heart? What did we all not want to remember?

What really happened? Saying these unsaid things, asking questions that would lead us to know what we did not want to know, and remembering the willfully forgotten things tears away the gauze, allowing the truth to heal.

Sifting through where we have come from helps us understand where we are going. Taking a fix on the things we have done and the things we have left undone gives us clues to who we are and who, for better or worse, we are becoming.

For each of us the task remains to inquire into which unsaid things need yet to be said. What unsaid things need not be said but merely remembered, acknowledged, embraced? This, too, is part of the reunion process. This, too, supports persistent Belonging.

For it is the skills of understanding, curiosity, and remembering that create empathy and compassion. Remembering makes love safe and allows for compassion to take its place in our hearts.

Compassion is enhanced by forgiveness. "You will begin to forgive the world," Tennessee Williams's psychiatrist told him, "when you forgive your father."

The world, perhaps, but also your mother. In forgiving my father for his disappearances, I came to an even deeper understanding of, and developed greater empathy for, my mother. Embracing the whole of me meant embracing the whole of even those who hurt me. Mom's illness may have pushed away my love, but she also got me those sneakers. Both stories are true.

And that acceptance—that a person can be both loving and cruel, that we can both crave their affection and recoil from their violence—makes it possible for me to see both of my parents not as wounded children but as adults, incomplete, insecure in their own Belonging, but nevertheless my ancestors. With this capacity to welcome them into my life, all parts of them, all their stories pouring forth, I reunite with the whole of them. Through this reunion, love, safety, and Belonging flourish.

"All flourishing is mutual," writes Robin Wall Kimmerer. If it's not mutual, it's not flourishing. If it's not flourishing, it's not safe. Acceptance is Belonging made manifest. Inclusion, if it's not safe, is not love. If it's not love, it's not Belonging. Belonging is always safe for it must always be mutual.

Now, knowing what I needed to know about to whom I belong, what their lives might have been, and reuniting with the forgotten, unclaimed parts of myself, I am better able to live into my moral and ethical responsibilities as a man with the power that comes from privilege. I am better able to dedicate myself to systemic Belonging precisely because I remember who I am, from whom I am descended, and to where I belong.

How might you take a fix on your own life? Consider giving yourself the gift of time alone, with little more than a pen and some paper. What memories are in your dreams? What stories of Belonging, as well as the threats to such Belonging, lay hidden in the half-recalled stories of your childhood, as well as that of your parents and grandparents?

If journaling doesn't appeal to you, go for a walk—possibly with a relative. Walk shoulder to shoulder, allow your bodies to find and keep pace with each other so that you may feel the safety of resonance with someone whose story may be similar enough. Share, with no objective other than to share, the stories that shaped your perceptions of love, safety, and, mostly, Belonging. See what this shared re-membering surfaces for you. Here are some questions to consider:

- What do I allow myself to remember?
- What was safer to have forgotten?
- How does it serve me, my family, my organization to have forgotten aspects of our origin?
- What parts of me may have been disowned by choosing not to remember?
- As I consider the things unsaid, what clues might I discover about who I am and, for a clue to who we are, who, for better or worse, I am becoming?
- Lastly, and looking forward, how would I like to be remembered?

PART II

Belonging to
Each Other

CHAPTER 5

The Wages of Separation

Within the walls of separateness death keeps watch.
—HOWARD THURMAN, *JESUS AND THE DISINHERITED*

We fly the flag at half-mast every week. Each week, another shooting. Each week, it seems, we bear witness to horrific manifestations of our deep fear of the Other: worshippers in churches, temples, and synagogues murdered because of how and to whom they pray. Or sometimes it's revelers in a nightclub murdered because of who and how they love.

Sometimes it's supermarket shoppers—perhaps a Black grandmother picking out produce—targeted because the shooter believed lies about white people being "replaced." Sometimes it's students—college, high school, middle school, fourth grade, or, God help us, kindergarteners, preparing for summer break. And sometimes it's an unarmed Black man stopped for a traffic violation or killed because the hoodie he was wearing, even the Skittles candies he was carrying, seemed threatening.

Pacing San Francisco's Embarcadero this morning, hearing the gulls screech and wail, I gather my thoughts for the work before me. How am I to speak of the costs of Othering and, by extension, the importance of systemic Belonging? As the ferries fan out across the bay, I recall the words of the apostle Paul: "For the wages of sin is death."

In this moment, with the crisp springtime air filling the bright sky, I wonder about our sins. What sins have we committed—what sins do we commit daily—that demand we pay this wage?

And more, despite the wages paid, what benefits do we derive from such sins? How have we—each of us, all of us— been complicit in, and, more importantly, benefited from, the conditions of the world we say we don't want?

Despite our protestations to the contrary, horrors persist. Through my years in analysis, I learned that behaviors persist in the individual because they serve some benefit however shameful, disowned, or denied.

Despite the myths we tell ourselves about ourselves, such behaviors also persist within our communities and our organizations. Despite our stated aspirations to increase representation and inclusion, to share equity and, thereby, increase love, safety, and Belonging for all, the walls of separation remain as high as ever. Perhaps even higher.

We live in an era when politicians and others in power accuse the other side of being agents of a nefarious Other. We live in a time when those seeking to gain and hold power call for secession, separation, and disunity, wielding systemic Othering as a political weapon.

Morality demands that we ask who benefits from separation, disunity, and its attendant violence.

Even more, the better angels of our collective nature demand that we ask what actions we are willing to take, what we are willing to give up that may make us feel loved, safe, and that *we* belong—so that a fourth grader can come home from a last day of school with a ribbon of recognition and not the trauma of having watched a friend, a cousin, or a teacher being murdered?

Morality demands that we inquire about complicity, benefits, and our willingness to take a stand. Those who hold less power than we do are asking us to account for our lack of action. This is why more than half of our employees are looking to CEOs, for example, to take a stand against division and separation and for Belonging. This is why so many are walking out of offices or striking for days, for weeks. Perhaps it'd help if we thought of these loud protests as the voices of the fierce-as-fuck better angels of our collective nature. Perhaps like my daughter, they are simply holding us accountable for creating the world we say we want.

It's not enough to be pious allies, these fierce angels sing—we must be willing to risk our significance.

What changes are we who hold power willing to endure, what loss are *you* willing to withstand, so that the world we know *must be* can be? What are you willing to recollect and regard, however painful, so that others may feel that they belong?

Recall the teachings of the philosopher, theologian, and activist Howard Thurman. Speaking of the force behind the hateful violence that can leave elderly churchgoing Taiwanese immigrants, Black grandmothers shopping for fruit, and tiny fourth graders excitedly awaiting summer dead, he preached: "It is clear, then, that this fear, which served originally as a safety device, a kind of protective mechanism for the weak, finally becomes death for the self."

The device that keeps us safe—the mechanism that protects us—is the fear-filled belief that the Other is a threat.

Protection and safety "turns executioner," driving us further and further apart. Fear of the Other is killing us. Beyond the walls of separateness, death stalks.

Separation, division, apartheid, and segregation all insult our primordial humanity and basic goodness. All forms of segregation—be it misogyny, xenophobia, homophobia, transphobia, anti-Semitism, classism, nationalism, racism, as well as fundamentalist, reductionist thinking that defines whole classes and cohorts of people as dangerous, dirty, and inhuman—are sins. There is no denying it; Othering is sinful.

Every instantiation of Othering rips apart any chance of Belonging. Othering supports supremacy, patriarchy, and the most extractive, exploitive aspects of capitalism. The sin of Othering manifests, for example, in enforced diaspora—a separation from the land and people to whom one has always belonged—by using degradation, war, genocidal ethnic cleansing, poverty, famine, as well as political, economic, or religious persecution. Such are the conditions we often say we don't want. Yet they benefit someone. Some pay the wages of separation while others reap the benefits.

Such setting apart—whether it's setting adrift flotillas of refugees from Vietnam, Haiti, or the northern coast of Africa seeking safety for themselves and their loved ones; or the immigrant "caravans" that politicians trumped up in their divisive, power-hungry, exploitative cries to "build the wall" on the southern border of the United States—tears people from their roots. Sin abounds in diaspora. It is the sinful torture, for example, of mothers in Guatemala, or the Rohingya in Myanmar, that is then exacerbated by the sinful treatment when they seek refuge. Tortured, beaten down, and Othered at home, they seek shelter only to find themselves tortured, beaten down, and Othered far from their birthplaces.

Disinherited and dispossessed, hungry at home and abroad, the flotilla of the rootless, landless encounters the hungry ghost settlers—colonizers whose only bulwark against their own fears of loss is an incessant demand for more. More land. More "freedom"—from the burdens of caring for and about others. More money—extracting pounds of flesh along with ore and oil from the earth.

All while ceaselessly offering less: less shelter, less food, and less clothing. The beatitudes of Christ notwithstanding, we treat the stranger, the Other, as a threat to our own love, safety, and Belonging.

Such sins are not merely against God but against humanity itself. They defile us. They degrade the very means of our development as a species. They assault the organ that distinguishes us from so many other beings: our compassionate heart.

But separation and segregation, as ubiquitous as they may be, are not fated. Division and dismemberment are choices. Indeed, for some, that choice is conscious. Some choose to see themselves, their tribe, as separate and distinct. Masters who are above all others. Think of the dark shadow behind the myth of American exceptionalism. Seeing ourselves as distinct, apart, and above the baser expressions of humanity means we are protected from criticism, incapable of systemically Othering, incapable of living less than the fullest expression of our aspirational values. The myth proclaims: "We are better than you."

Such myths protect us from the fear of being subsumed or

replaced by the Other. Not spoken aloud is the usefulness of our metaphors. That which is distinct dissolves into the melting pot of assimilation, further separating individuals from their past, their language, their culture, and the land of their ancestors. Separation from those to whom we belonged, and their stories and their lives, in service of moving into and within the dominant cohort. Assimilation in service of the supremacy of whiteness. Disunion in service of a fable of equal opportunity, exceptional freedoms, and a simulacrum of unity.

"Beloved community is formed not by the eradication of difference but by its affirmation," wrote bell hooks in *Killing Rage: Ending Racism*. It is formed "by each of us claiming the identities and cultural legacies that shape who we are and how we live in the world."

For many of us living in the safe confines of an "exceptional" dominant class, the choice to participate in systemically Othering, and maintaining this death-inducing separation, is unconscious. It is a choice, nonetheless, and one that is rationalized with a sophistication common to our wily protective ego. Separation, says our ego, becomes a "protective mechanism" meant to guard us against the threats presented by those from the margins, those not in a dominator class, the Other, as when a fear of immigrants is cloaked by a self-declared patriotism attaching love, safety, and Belonging to a mythology constructed by our ego; we then fight like hell to maintain that construct. We fear losing status in some twisted theory about replacement, so we close our minds to the Others' cultural identities and rights to love, safety, and Belonging. We fear losing power over the other, and so we choose to allow destruction—to them as well as to ourselves—over the safety of a difference-affirming beloved community.

WHAT MUST WE CLAIM?

When I was younger, I struggled with the concept of inter-dependence; depending on another always felt risky. Perhaps my reluctance to rely on another, like the myths of exceptionalism, protected me from being subsumed by the Other. Merging with the Other frightened me; it threatened the tenuous hold I had on my individuality. It seemed best not to need anyone.

One day I shared this belief with a Buddhist teacher. He waggled his head, chuckling. He smiled gently and held up his hand, spreading wide his fingers. "Where do the individual fingers end?" he asked. "Where does the hand begin?" Pointing to each finger, opening and closing his hand, he asked, "See how the fingers work together? See how together they *are* the hand?" The individual exists as a manifestation of the collective whole. The interdependence of each finger doesn't threaten anything.

Losing sight of collective interdependent community increases the tension between the individual and the collective. That tension is so troubling, so frightening, that we often vigorously, viciously defend "our" collective, our "tribe," against the Other. To protect the hand, we sever the finger. Holding the tension between the individual and collective needs is, perhaps, among the most difficult challenges for those of us inspired to lead.

The wage we pay for losing that tension is the loss of a hand that could create and build a beloved world, one in which community is based on touch, connection, love, and beyond racialized identities that separate identities rooted in known ground and the lives of our ancestors. We lose the right and responsibilities of empathetic connection, the birthright gift of compassion. We sever fingers, and blood flows.

Worse still, that which has been severed remains lifeless flesh and bone, questioning its worthiness of love, wholly unsafe, and cut off from life-giving Belonging.

Both individuals and the collective—the unsevered fingers and the hand—pay the wages of separation and segregation, from those condemned for fighting systemic Othering to those who endured the Middle Passage; from refugees displaced by greed and hunger, or political or religious oppression, to children who may one day be murdered in a classroom in Uvalde, Texas; Sandy Hook, Connecticut; Parkland, Florida; or on a street in Ferguson, Missouri. Or under the knee of a cop on a street in Minneapolis, Minnesota. Or in her bedroom, in her apartment, home from a long day as a technician in an emergency room hospital, in Louisville, Kentucky.

Again and again, the wages of Othering manifest in severing. Behind walls of separation the Other may be interned as an enemy alien; may be held in the murder factories of Nazi-occupied Europe, the gulags of Siberia, the killing fields of Cambodia, the refugee camps in Buddhist Myanmar, or the reeducation camps for China's Uighurs.

Time and again we see genocidal policies manifested in the denial of food, clothing, care, and shelter—all rationalized by dehumanization and the call to protect the dominant group. Time and again we see genocide in service to those with the power. When we look at our prisons, detention centers, and even our refugee camps, can we see who benefits from such conditions?

The frightened masses, even within the dominant class,

have their fears stoked and transformed into a paranoia that says vaccines are an effort by the powerful to control the common person, that the rich are a part of a global cabal whose loyalties lie in a religious affiliation, that the poor are lazy, that migrants are job stealers, and that democracy needs to be defended with a storming of the US Capitol one January morning.

The truly powerful exploit such fears to maintain their power. Fear of the loss of status and power leads to the maintenance of myths of patriotic exceptionalism. Fear of falling out of dominance fuels an uncritical, unimaginative, closed-minded rejection of deeper inquiries into who we all are, to whom we have belonged, and how we can move to the systemic Belonging of beloved community.

As a life-giving vaccine became the object of life-threatening lies, so, too, life-giving inquiries into our shared past and a more honest understanding of our present—inquiries such as critical race theory, which could have provided a blueprint for a future systemic Belonging—become bogeymen.

The perceived threat to whiteness fuels a steady stream of murders of marginalized people. This is the death that keeps watch over our divided, dismembered body politic. These are the wages of separation.

Hope flags and spirits sag in the onslaught of these wages to be paid. I am reminded of writer and teacher Parker Palmer's notion of the tragic gap, the gap between the world as it is and the world as it could be. "We are called to stand in the gap," he teaches, the place between irrelevant idealism and corrosive cynicism.

I am seeking the resilience to move from heartbreak and

mourning to the equanimity that comes from actions that heal. Once more, I enter the room called Remember to reunite with the source of love and strength.

THE BELONGING OF A BEST FRIEND

There's nothing like the love of a best friend. Mine was Marcus, and he lived just next door. A chain-link fence separated our backyards, but nothing kept us apart. From early morning, when the normally hot asphalt was cool enough for us to lie on our bellies and shoot bottle caps filled with Crayola crayon wax, through to the late afternoon, when the bees buzzed in and out of the flowers, and finally until the white-light, fluorescent streetlamps would click on, signaling the end of the day, we were together.

His little brother, Mark, would do his best to hang with us. Mark and Marcus had different mothers but they were both named for their father. Like so many kids on the streets of Brooklyn, Mark was never without his Spaldeen. He'd bounce, bounce, and bounce as he shifted from foot to foot. Like so many little brothers, he'd often beg to play with us. "Come on, guys . . . let's play stickball." Bounce. Bounce. Bounce. "Guys, come on, doncha wanna play?" Bounce. Bounce. Bounce.

Mark and my little brother, John, would peel off and play stoop ball. Mark would face the stoop and slam the pink rubber ball against the steps in front of our houses, John in the street, mindful of cars coming down the block, would catch the ball, and, depending on where the ball was caught, it would count as a single, double, triple, or the very rare home run. ("Car!" someone, anyone, up and down the street would yell, a warning for everyone to move.)

Marcus's family came north from Alabama. His father worked as a conductor on the subway. Marcus was Black. I am white. Those were the facts. He preferred Jolly Ranchers and Charleston Chews and knew more about sex than I did. More facts.

In the Brooklyn of my youth, the local form of apartheid— segregated schools, housing, playgrounds, and skully courts— was fueled by economic policies such as block busting, where mendacious real estate agents took advantage of the fears of the Other to create wedges in communities; this caused the white families to sell their homes at below-market rates, which then allowed the real estate agents to charge Black families above-market prices for those very same homes. Separation in the service of capitalism. Those who benefited hid behind the desks of Realtors and bankers.

The bankers and real estate agents who benefited from this odious form of systemic Othering—the manipulative community-destroying tactics of block busting, redlining, and restrictive racial and religious covenants designed to under-mine any chance of beloved community from developing— also encouraged a fight for survival. "Their" streets became dangerous to "us." "Our" streets dangerous to "them."

And the forces that had Othered the descendants of the for-merly enslaved shifted, and those descendants of immigrants from Europe—Italian, Irish, Jewish, and German kids— moved into the minority. Kids who looked like my siblings and me became the target of intimidation by kids who looked like Marcus. Walking to St. Jerome School, wearing my maroon uniform jacket, white shirt with maroon tie, and gray slacks with a maroon stripe on the outer edges of my pant legs, I'd be stopped by a hand on a chest: "Gotta quarter?"

Most days and sometimes every day, a hand on my chest and the inevitable question: "Gotta quarter?"

Then one night Dad went out for his nightly beer run and was mugged for his beer money. The beating Dad received broke one of his legs in several places and left him with a slight limp for the rest of his life: a limp and a terror of the night and the Other. We moved away from East Twenty-Sixth Street over Christmas break. Within weeks we'd left Flatbush, left the house that Grandpa owned, and settled into a new neighborhood, Bensonhurst, where we were no longer in the minority. I don't recall a single Black kid at our new school, Saints Simon & Jude Elementary School, in the parish named for the same saints. When we moved, Marcus was down in Alabama visiting relatives.

I never said good-bye.

One day we were split up; the inseparable were separated. There's a boy inside me who thinks it's his fault. In the quiet of the evening, when I think about my life, I tell myself I abandoned my best friend. I miss him so much.

That move, that separation, rooted as it was in the violence in our community, made me feel my whiteness as I never had before. I finally saw my difference from Marcus, and that difference frightened me.

A "VICTORY FOR WHITE LIFE"

As I write these words, the streets of America are once more filled with protestors, this time resisting the decision by the Supreme Court to overturn *Roe v. Wade*, turning back the clock on nearly fifty years of the right to personal choice. As I write

THE WAGES OF SEPARATION | 115

these words, a video of Illinois congresswoman Mary Miller circulates. In it, she stands next to the former president Donald Trump and thanks him for his choices for Supreme Court justices.

She then calls the decision to dismantle a woman's right to seek the healthcare she chooses a "victory for white life." With that phrase, she let slip what many have long understood is the root of the drive to control women's lives. Fears of changing demographics—a phrase that sounds innocuous and, perhaps, even scientific—are closely aligned with the same nativist, white supremacist thinking that Othered our ancestors.

This "victory for white life" means the further erosion of the rights of those who might be nonwhite, cementing the connection with systemic racism. The country's long history of nativist anti-Black, anti-nonwhite, anti-immigrant Othering updated and revived during the post-Trump presidency and revitalized in an abhorrent America First movement with echoes of Nazi Germany.

The movement stoked fears of the racist, supremacist theory of replacement of white Americans. Americans who ironically are often the descendants of those whose own status was ambiguous, a state between white and nonwhite.

This painful and repeated pattern of exploiting fears in service of populist power grabs is so common in the United States that the prescient irony of Sinclair Lewis's novel *It Can't Happen Here* is lost on most white Americans. Huey Long and Joe McCarthy reborn as Donald Trump; reanimated and reenergized with Islamophobia and expressions of anti-Semitism inherent in chants of "America First" and "Make America Great Again."

Lost in the haze of such fearmongering is Langston Hughes's dream to "Let America Be America Again," even if it was never America to him and the millions who labored, lived, and loved within the walls of that separating pattern, with death keeping watch.

There's a through line that connects anti-Black racism, white supremacy, patriarchy, the fear of the Other (be they gay, trans, immigrant, nonwhite, non-Christian, or anyone who doesn't fit the heteronormative fable of America). This line is straight and undeniable for those willing to question the ways their lack of seeing has led them to be complicit in, and benefit from, a world where the majority feel unloved, unsafe, and as if they do not belong.

"Three plagues, three contagions, threaten the world," observed Polish journalist Ryszard Kapuściński in *Imperium*, his history of the end days of the former Soviet Union. The plagues of nationalism, racism, and religious fundamentalism all share a common denominator, and anyone stricken by one of these plagues is "beyond reason." "In his head burns a sacred pyre that awaits only its sacrificial victims. Every attempt at calm conversation will fail. He doesn't want a conversation, but a declaration that you agree with him, admit that he is right, join the cause." Minds infected by these plagues spin around one subject: the threatening Other, the enemy.

These plagues reinforce one another. They are woven together by that through line that starts with the myths of American exceptionalism and sameness, denies the realities of our ancestors, and runs straight through systemic oppression and voter suppression, the denial of gender-affirming healthcare, and a complex of forced-birth restrictions and laws—the imposition of theocratic morals cloaked in false intellectualism and arguments about the original intent of the framers of the Constitution.

The line passes by supermarkets in Buffalo and Boulder; gay nightclubs in Orlando and Colorado Springs; synagogues in Pittsburgh and New York; churches in Charleston and Sutherland Springs; a gurdwara, where Sikh faithful pass through the doorway to the Guru, in Oak Creek; and a discount store in El Paso.

The line manifests in feet on necks, holding some of us down while others enjoy privileges that they believe are their right based on their gender or race, such identities merely the happenstances of constructs adopted in service of white supremacy and patriarchy. They "got" to be white, cisgender, and male, and therefore they have a right to rest their feet on the necks of others.

"I ask no favor for my sex," said the late Supreme Court justice Ruth Bader Ginsburg in a documentary about her efforts to fight the Othering of people who identify as women. "All I ask of our brethren is that they take their feet off our necks."

This through line tilts our economic and political policies toward the rich and away from the dispossessed and wretched of the earth. It secures their power through dehumanization, through the deemphasis on compassion, as well as a fetish-like attachment to guns. It is powered by narrow, fundamentalist, overly religious, and arguably amoral belief systems. It ends in fascist totalitarianism.

I don't know if the stakes could be any higher. I can't see how the wages could be any greater. We need this great reunion to interrupt the through line. Indeed, beyond knowing our ancestors and their stories, beyond seeing our story in the Other, reunion demands that we see the ways dehumanizing

Othering is reinforced repeatedly by seemingly disparate, disconnected actions. We need to see, acknowledge, and internalize all the connections so we might alter the outcome.

This is what those fierce angels protesting ask of us. This is what the majority not only of our employees but of our country demands of us. For this is what our children will hold us accountable: the end of that through line.

RIDING THE THROUGH LINE TO WHITENESS

With the passing of time, I see more clearly my family's move from Flatbush to Bensonhurst. We rode the through line of systemic Othering and worked our way toward a greater sense of whiteness, realizing the dream of my ancestors. Our whiteness proof that we overcame the view of the southern Italians and Irish as inhuman dogs, incapable and undeserving of citizenship, and better off going back to whence we came, where we belonged. Our movement from Flatbush to Bensonhurst completed the family's move to whiteness.

The truth, though, was that the policies consciously designed to spur homeownership and the development of an economic middle class created further separation and division.

Newly created suburbs in places such as Long Island, New Jersey, and even within the City of New York itself on Staten Island were the places to which our white neighbors fled. The creation of restrictive housing covenants intended to maintain the illusion of property values was a protective mechanism that resulted in neighborhoods and cities being defined as "bad." The euphemism I grew up hearing was "turned."

"Did you hear that parish is turning?"

Turning. Meaning moving from white to nonwhite and, therefore, becoming unsafe for white people. The irony of my ancestors being deemed part of the same force of "turning" a neighborhood was lost to the fables and gauzy myths of time.

"When I move / into a neighborhood," wrote Langston Hughes in his 1949 poem "Restrictive Covenants," "folks fly." Folks—especially those recently accepted as white folks—flew, landing in a better economic state. The land of opportunity closed off to those left behind.

By exploiting the long-standing, simmering, and seething tensions that pitted new immigrants such as my grandparents from southern Italy (indeed anyone from the non-Nordic, non-Saxon, non-Alpine parts of Europe) against those who'd always been here (such as the descendants of the Indigenous peoples) as well as those whose ancestors were brought to North America as enslaved people, they not only grew rich but prevented the new arrivals from using homeownership to accumulate wealth. That privilege, using homeownership to create intergenerational wealth that might then be used to educate children and grandchildren, was a touchstone of the European immigrant experience.

We, my family as well as Marcus's, lived the tension implicit in Hughes's poem. That tension separated friends who were closer than brothers. Separated boys who were supposed to attend each other's wedding, bear witness to the births of each other's children, and be the pallbearers at each other's funeral.

My family left my birthplace, and I began seeking a place to which I might belong.

In the pursuit of my family's safety, we lost culture. We lost language. We lost a connection to place and forgot the true stories of our ancestors, disregarding their lived experiences, leaving them as hungry ghosts. We lost the narrative of who we were, and through that loss we were disinherited from who we could be. We buried the safety of our Belonging under the weight of whiteness.

THE PRICE OF WHITENESS

In his essay "The Price of the Ticket," James Baldwin admonishes that we must go back to where it all started, to go back as far as one can, to travel our road again. "Sing or shout or testify or keep it to yourself: but *know whence we came*." Unfortunately, though, knowing whence we came, traveling the roads of our past lives and those of our hungry ghost ancestors, "is precisely what the generality of white Americans cannot afford to do," he says. "They do not know how to do it."

Further, he adds, "They come through Ellis Island, where *Giorgio* becomes *Joe*, *Pappavasiliu* becomes *Palmer*, *Evangelos* becomes *Evans*, *Goldsmith* becomes *Smith* or *Gold*, and *Avakian* becomes *King*. So with a painless change of name, and in the twinkling of an eye, one becomes a white American."

Later the price of that ticket, the wage of a separation not from others but from oneself and from one's source of Belonging, is paid. The currency is heartache. Heartache, and the critical lack of safety in whatever Belonging one holds. He adds, "The missing identity aches."

The missing identity, the ghostly disregard of our ancestors, the heartache of lost language and place, as well as the fearful, tenuous nature of our grasp on the safety of whiteness, prevents those of us who hold power from seeing the disinherited all around us. It fuels our complicity in creating

the systemic conditions of Othering that we vehemently declare we do not want to see in the world. It severs us from
the five-fingered grasp of interdependence, the empathy of
knowing that my story is your story, and that your story is
my story.

The price my ancestors paid was nothing near the price others paid—Asian immigrants, Indigenous folks, and the sons
and daughters of the enslaved, for example, continue to bear
the burden of this movement toward whiteness. We see this
in no-knock warrants ending in a young woman dying from
police bullets. We see this in a mass incarceration that mocks
the supposed freedom implicit in the Thirteenth Amendment.
We see this in relentless attacks on scholarly analyses such as
critical race theory that would have us look unflinchingly at
the myths of sameness, colorblindness, and exceptionalism.

Our neighbors, our friends, our loved ones pay the price
when they are shopping while Black, walking to the produce
market while being an elderly immigrant from China, or
seeking gender-affirming care as a questioning teen seeking
only to feel loved, safe, and as if they belong in a community
and culture threatened by anything that doesn't fit a binary
narrative.

The price of that ticket, the wages of the resulting separation, are paid in bullets and bullying, at torchlit marches
echoing with shouts about not being replaced, and in the daily
tirades of threats seen in a Haitian father or Mexican mother
ferrying their children across the Rio Grande.

The price of the ticket of our unique differences dissolving
in the melting pot of assimilation, where "they" become "us,"
and therefore better, more human, than those who flee oppressive famine, political repression, and human deprivation.

When I was a boy, the summer after we'd moved from Flatbush to the Italian American area of Bensonhurst, I was out on the streets with my friends. Paulie, Patty, Stevie, and I wandering the dark and cooling Avenue X, not far from McDonald Avenue, the border between "our" Italian neighborhood and "their" Jewish neighborhood. We passed a boy, not much different from us, who called us "zipperheads" for the way most of us wore our hair, fluffed up and parted down the middle like Tony Manero, the character played by John Travolta in *Saturday Night Fever*. I laughed it off because, unlike my friends, I never wore my hair like that. (Okay, I did. But only once when I went to a school dance and wore a powder-blue three-piece suit and danced to Van McCoy's "The Hustle." But never again.)

As I stood there laughing, the boy called me a dago and a Guinea. I had no idea what those words meant, but I knew they were bad.

Dago, a corruption of the name Diego, was applied first to Spanish and Portuguese immigrants to the United States and later came to be used (by Theodore Roosevelt, as well as the boy on Avenue X) for Italians. *Guinea*, the word for the British gold coin, was, in turn, associated with the slave trade in people from the Guinea coastal region of Africa. It evolved to stand for the enslaved people themselves and eventually was applied to the enslaved, the formerly enslaved, and finally to those whose immigrant status left their whiteness ambiguous.

Instead of slurs, these words could have served as empathetic bridges, paragraphs in the mutual stories of Belonging. Instead, they became bricks in the walls of separateness.

Such slurs, though, reinforce the tenuous nature of the

movement of immigrants to the relative safety of white Americanness.

The myth of exceptionalism, the fables of truth, justice, and the American way, the gaslighting that begins with "all men are created equal." *Gaslighting* because every time we utter those words we stumble. What did that phrase really mean? All property owners? Whites only? Men only? In 1790, Congress passed a law whose meaning was debated well into the twentieth century. Naturalization—that is, citizenship—was open only to white immigrants. What happened to "all men are created equal"?

In a liberal, privileged response ignoring the gaslighting, we stammer and stumble, trying to insert the phrase "all people" into the founding documents that, try as our myths might, fail to conceal their role in maintaining white supremacist, patriarchal, and classist structures inherent in the land of the free and home of the brave.

In saying these things out loud, I run the risk of being accused of betraying others like myself. Indeed, I run the risk of attack by those who would impose a version of Christianity that is nativist, supremacist, and patriarchal. In other words, nothing like the brown, Aramaic-speaking Jesus who preached a sermon at the Mount of Beatitude on the Korazim Plateau.

But to live up to the exhortation of my antiracist daughter, to be more than an ally, to be an active co-conspirator, I must be willing to risk that which I love to see the world I want to call into creation—a world where all people, however they identify; whomever and however they love; whatever their roots—and feel the embrace of love, safety, and Belonging. The felt sense of inclusion.

If I am "canceled," then so be it. Jesus, the Buddha, the Prophet, Socrates, Marcus Aurelius—these elders taught me better. These elders taught us all better than our actions and our world would have us believe.

The disconnect between the true teachings of our elders and the world as it is spawns an evil manifested in coffins for fourth graders.

The banality of this evil—the evil of moving toward the safety of whiteness as a protective mechanism that maintains systemic Othering—is rooted in the negative space left by those missing elders and forgotten ancestors. To paraphrase Baldwin, the only sure path to truer inclusivity is to know from whence one came. Perhaps then we might know to whom we belong. Then we might let go of the fear of no longer being safe—one of the consequences of our ambiguous hold on the privilege of whiteness. And finally, we might be co-conspirators in the creating and maintaining of systemic Belonging for all.

I'm not usually this strident. I'm reluctant to be polemical; it's against my training as a coach, where my task is to ask the right questions. But the banality of this evil demands a strong, unequivocable response. My words are my best tools to lift the weightiness of that which holds us down; this is the best way I know to support the world I want to see come into being. I have words. I have language. And I have a platform. Like the elders who have inspired me, it is my duty to use these tools well.

THE PURSUIT OF WEIGHTLESSNESS

It is my duty, as Baldwin wrote, to do my first works over and reexamine everything.

Amid the pandemic, when strife and separation were exacerbated by the toxic, hungry ghost leadership of those in power, thousands took to the streets to protest this murder. Many saw this murder as part of the long and tragic chain of murders dating back centuries, dating back at least to 1619.

For a few weeks, at least, many were willing to do their first works over.

I'd met Philippe Celestin shortly before the murder of George Floyd. We'd connected via social media, and, like others before, he saw his own story in the stories I'd shared in *Reboot*. "Given the nature of your journey," he said, "I'd be honored to have a conversation with someone who 'gets it,' and by 'it' I mean the power of stories and Belonging."

"At this moment in our country's history," added Philippe, whose mother is white and whose father is a Black Haitian immigrant, "I need conversations like that." He continued, "I suppose we all do."

Until he'd pointed it out, I didn't realize how right he was. Until he'd written, I didn't realize how much I needed to share stories of Belonging. Until that moment, I hadn't understood that my stories—told from the vantage point of my own broken-open-hearted journey to the warriorship of elderhood—created the ground of Belonging for others. Until that moment, I hadn't realized how much we need to hear each other's longing to belong.

The calls and emails with Philippe increased over the next few weeks. A teacher and an artist, he was in the middle of a life transition. Leaving a charter school in DC and focusing his time more on a nonprofit, after-school program called the Creative School for mostly Black and brown kids ("Queens and Kings," as they call them) in the DC area. The program, founded by Philippe's friend Marshall Pollard, helps kids find agency through creative expression, healing from the trauma of gun violence, and Belonging through beloved community. Philippe and Marshall are two good men working to activate and unleash the force of love and life so that fewer Queens and Kings might die.

In one of our calls, speaking mostly about his transition, Philippe mentioned that Marshall and another friend, Mostafa Wafa, an immigrant from Egypt and a graduate student in DC, were all drawn to my story. We agreed to form a small group of friends, peers really, who would come together to share, to open our hearts, to do our first works over.

To that initial group, I brought my friend and fellow coach Carl Desir, as well as Ashanti Branch, Shawn Dove, and Gaurav Manchanda.

Months before, Carl and I had spoken about how much the themes in my work resonated with him. As I mention earlier in this volume, Carl cried in one of our calls because—as his sister explained to his family—"He'd been seen." My work over the years, both my writing and my support for entrepreneurs in general, had brought Gaurav, Shawn, and Ashanti into my life.

Gaurav, a social entrepreneur dedicated to making a positive dent in the universe, is a young father sorting through his place in the world.

Shawn, after decades of creating opportunity for others, was sunsetting the nonprofit he'd founded, the Corporation for Black Male Achievement, and beginning to focus his efforts on writing a memoir, *I Too Am America*. Taking its title from the Langston Hughes poem "I, Too," the book tells the story of Shawn's growing up in New York in the 1970s. Once again each of us finding resonance in the other's story.

Ashanti's work with young Black and brown boys, mostly

in Northern California, was profiled in the 2015 film *The Mask You Live In*. The film details the work of the Ever Forward Club, an organization Ashanti founded in 2004 while he was a math teacher at a high school in San Lorenzo, California. One of his signature workshops is to help young men see what's behind the masks they wear, the ones we all wear.

At one of our first meetings, we named ourselves the Warriors, in honor of the image of the broken-open-hearted warrior so crucial to the work of moving into our fullest potential. And with that the masks came down. After a simple check-in, where we each told the truth of how we were doing, the truth of our struggles that first summer of COVID as we witnessed many trying to do their first works over, these brave, beautiful men shook with the tears of being seen, of being held, and of Belonging.

"Men of color," Carl explained to me, "we don't talk like this—not in front of other men of color."

"Neither do white men," I added. Of course, that's part of the problem; that's part of the wages of separation.

The masks stayed down, and the weight bearing down on each of us lifted a little as we shared stories of our lives. I spoke of my efforts to write this book as a response to my own need to do my first works over. Mostafa shared a memory of the way his grandmother smelled: "Like heaven," he said, remembering and smiling.

And he shared what it had been like when he and so many others had risked their lives (and others had paid with their lives) when they'd joined thousands in Tahrir Square in 2011 to protest the brutal regime of Hosni Mubarak. Mask off, he could weep with the memories of bullets hitting his friends and feeling the embrace of his grandmother.

I asked these brave, broken-open men, "What's it like to share like this?"

"It's the pursuit of weightlessness," spoke the usually rather quiet Marshall. "It's weightless."

The weight of Othering lifted by the power of seeing ourselves in the others' stories. The pursuit being the goal of systemic Belonging and beloved community. The weightlessness of men sharing their suffering and giving birth to the felt sense of inclusion: love, safety, and Belonging. The reunion process extending to and among men of different backgrounds, faiths, and experiences, united in their grief and hope.

With those meetings, I missed Marcus even more.

Seeing that one's own story is the story of the other—an essential part of the reunion process—can repair some of the wages of separation. The fundamental and unshakable truth that your story is my story advances the natural state of grace and empathy that is our birthright as humans.

This is what these warrior men of color taught this white man. These men, these warriors, give me hope. They, like so many others, compel me to try.

I try despite knowing I may fail. But I can't be a bridge if I am unwilling to be trodden on. I must feel the dirt and mud of potential imperfection; I must risk the privilege that comes from white supremacy. I must be willing, as poet Dawna Markova says, "to risk my significance."

I shared some of what I was endeavoring to do with this book with my friend, the Buddhist teacher and activist Konda Mason. A Black woman navigating the predominantly white world of American Buddhism, Konda affirmed that, in recalling my ancestors, I was headed in the right direction.

Echoing Baldwin, she said, "That's right. To go forward,

we must go back." To that wisdom, I'd add, to learn, we must be willing to err.

In the introduction, I wrote about being bold enough to be worthy of the look in my son Michael's eyes. Even more, I must be bold enough to be worthy of the trust of these good men and of all the people who, in finding resonance in my story, found articulation of their own. "Your story is my story" is not just a statement of empathy, of fingers on the same hand, it's a statement of understanding as well.

Poet Wendell Berry, in his book *The Hidden Wound*, wrote: "It may be the most significant irony in our history that racism," by separating us *into* races, has made us "not separate but in a fundamental way inseparable, not independent but dependent on each other, incomplete without each other, each needing desperately to understand and make use of the experience of the other."

LASTING CHANGE

What creates real, lasting change is marrying insightful awareness—stemming from straight, linear assertions that are clear—with the felt sense of what life would be like after the change, after the reunion. We need to feel our way past the defenses that cause us to be complicit in creating the world we say we do not want.

The reunion process works not only because it counters Othering, but because it reunites us with our innate sources of strength, with the innate sense of Belonging that our ancestors fought to secure for us. It reunites us with the intergenerational wisdom that can help us take our seat in the world.

What's needed for true reunion, and therefore lasting

transformation, are visceral somatic experiences coupled with repetition. Reverie, active imagination, art such as poetry—all drop people into their bodies, into their hearts. Then the energy that is stirred up becomes the fuel for transformation, connection, and reunion. This is why beauty and art are needed. Reunion, like welcoming the unwelcome, begins with a broken heart.

From whom have you been separated and why? What role might race or other identity have played in that separation? The loss of Marcus in my life felt, and still feels, like an open wound. Whose stories are your stories and how might seeing and re-membering those stories heal those wounds?

Consider another walk, this time with someone outside your typical circle of acquaintances. What of your own longing to belong might you hear in the other's longing?

Whose experiences do you need to understand, without which you might be incomplete? What do you need to do your first works over and foster the Belonging you desperately want to will into existence?

CHAPTER 6

Leadership and the Disinherited

The masses of men live with their backs constantly against the wall. They are the poor, the disinherited, the dispossessed.

—HOWARD THURMAN, *JESUS AND THE DISINHERITED*

Growing up, I rarely encountered anyone who'd been in-carcerated. There were, of course, the rough encounters with the law that might land someone (say, my brother, after being caught smoking weed) overnight in jail (when a father *may* have refused to bail out the brother for twenty-four hours to "teach him a lesson").

Still, I just didn't think of them, didn't see them. Those with their backs to the wall, knees on their necks, dispossessed of that which would give them love, safety, and Belonging—all these people were out of sight and out of mind.

My whiteness, and the power and privilege that came with it, allowed me to grow up, become educated, build a career (or two), become a father, fall in love, accumulate wealth that I could pass on to my children and my children's children, and to experience the world in safety with an unquestioned sense of Belonging. It also allowed me to place the incarcerated, the disinherited, and dispossessed—all those, really, whose necks were clamped down by knees—behind a gauzy myth of self-satisfied sympathy, safe from a dangerous discovery, that their story may not be so different from my story or those of my ancestors.

All that changed the day I read some journal entries from men in prison.

Years earlier, I'd recorded a series of videos that became part of a curriculum teaching entrepreneurship to some incarcerated people. The program aims to lower recidivism rates by teaching a different way to hustle. The videos helped the participants understand a bit more about their own leadership strengths. I still receive letters of gratitude from folks who've watched them.

The videos, though, were also an effective means for me to maintain my distance (and my safety). By speaking *at* the program participants, and not *with* them, I was able to feel sympathy for their experience. But the truth is I never looked into their hearts. I never really saw them, and when the day was done, I could forget about them.

That began to change, however, in the fall of 2021. More than a year after *Reboot* had been released, while I was beginning to feel my way into the writing of this book, I connected with a local group doing this work closer to my home in Colorado.

The program's participants read *Reboot* and responded to the journaling prompts at the end of each chapter—many of which were shared with me. Having gone first, having shared so much of my story, they then shared their stories. Knowing their stories, I began to see their lives.

"Like Jerry . . . ," and "Like the author . . . ," began so many entries. "I, too, played Monopoly," said one reader referring to the game I played with my mother as a boy. Another, too, like me "was number six of seven kids." Many were seen but not seen. All were found but not truly found out. All remained hidden, all the while hurting, their suffering safely tucked away and never addressed. I think of my friend Parker Palmer's assertion: "Violence is what happens when we don't know what to do with suffering."

Reading of the lives of men behind walls, I wondered again about my role, my responsibility, my complicity in—and benefit from—the mass dehumanization as one who holds power.

I have enormous power. For example, as an author, I've been given a platform from which to speak. Therefore, I am a leader. And if I am not using my leadership to lift knees off necks, to move the disinherited away from the wall and into the safe embrace of other humans, then what am I? I think of the heartbreaking teachings of Rabbi Hillel: "If I am only for myself, what am I?"

Leadership is only leadership when it is for those whose necks are under knees and whose backs are against the wall— the poor, the dispossessed, the disinherited. Howard Thurman wondered what it was that religion could offer the disinherited and called that question the "most important" religious quest of modern life.

The task of lifting those struck down, of making visible those who have been erased, of touching the untouchable and breaking down the castes that separate and cause so much death, is the most important *leadership* quest of modern life.

While it is true and good and right to ask what religion

holds for the disinherited, it's equally true and right to ask what leadership and power hold for the same people. How should those who have the privilege of power respond to the poor? How should those who hold the titles and sigils of leadership be with those who have been dispossessed and disinherited?

There's a hint in the word *religion*. Based on the Latin *religare*—to bind together, *religion* means to live up and into the obligation of a bond. What bond?

Well, first, the bond with the divine. But also the bond with each other, to overcome the walls of separateness.

The modern life quest of *religare*—this binding together—is to reunite that which has been cut off and out of our lives. To re-member those who have been dismembered and severed. To bring all, including the unseen and forgotten who are incarcerated, as well as the descendants of the Indigenous people whose lands were taken by unrelenting hungry ghosts yearning for more, the descendants of the enslaved whose labor built that which we hold as exceptional—this shining City Upon the Hill, the "huddled masses," not only those who've come from Europe but those who came and still come from Latin America and Asia.

I don't mean to imply a false equivalency between religious traditions and corporations. But there was a time when the world's religions were the engines of power: civic, political, economic, and existential. Indeed, there *was* a time and there still *is* a time when extractive capitalistic impulses served the institutional interests of religious entities and actively participated in millennia of systemic Othering.

As I write these words, Pope Francis has returned from a trip to Canada to apologize to the Indigenous First Nations peoples for the Catholic Church's role in the dehumanizing theft of culture and language and, in some cases, the lives of thousands of children of the disinherited there.

Indeed, as I write these words, members of the worldwide Society of Jesus (the "Jesuits") are struggling to live up to a promise made to distribute $100 million as reparations (inadequate as it may be) to the descendants of those enslaved and sold to create income for the economic expansion of the society in their misguided bid to spread the gospel.

And, as I write *these* words, two former judges have been ordered to pay $200 million in reparations to people, including children, whom they ordered to jail for minor crimes in a scheme through which they received kickbacks from for-profit prisons. The link between extractive capitalism maintaining systems of injustice and systemic Othering is shockingly clear, hiding in plain sight.

Still, there is the by-product of the age of capitalism: the ascendency of the corporation. Indeed, today corporate structures are rivaled only by nation-states in the powers they wield.

Given this reality, given the power of these institutions, what responsibilities come with that power? Let's imagine a world where businesses take up the mantle of Belonging, fulfilling the obligation of that bond to each other, to overcome the walls, indeed the ramparts, that separate us from one another.

What if the purpose of political and business leadership shifted from amassing wealth, extracting resources and labor, and maintaining itself to a higher purpose: *religare*. To bind together, to honor that bond by bringing together the disinherited and the ascendant and privileged into one beloved community.

A few weeks ago, on an otherwise uneventful day, I received notes of gratitude from two different readers. One is the CEO of a Fortune 100 company with thousands of employees. The other is an inmate on death row. Both men shared reactions to *Reboot*; both said, essentially, that my story is their story. By the power of a transitive relationship, each of their stories is the other's. Each of these men are members of the same beloved community.

What if the radical self-inquiry into the why of our leadership landed simply on community? What if the point of growing up and becoming a better human, and therefore a better leader, was to leave the world better than you found it? What if the purpose of the power of privilege was to return the lands and inheritances to the dispossessed and disinherited? What if the purpose of power was simply to bind us one to the other?

THE RESTRICTED LIVES OF THE DISINHERITED

I'm grateful that so much has been written about the effects of trauma on the body. The work of writers such as Bessel van der Kolk, Peter Levine, and Resmaa Menakem* helped me tremendously.

I'm grateful but also disappointed. Just as I have overlooked the lives of those incarcerated, just as I have failed to truly see the Othering of my ancestors and the ways their movement toward the safety, the sanctity of whiteness furthered white

---

* Their books—*The Body Keeps Score: Brain, Mind, and Body in the Healing of Trauma* (Kolk); *Waking the Tiger: Healing Trauma* (Levine); and *My Grandmother's Hands: Racialized Trauma and the Pathway to Mending Our Hearts and Bodies* (Menakem)—are part of a brilliant collection that explores the somatic experience of Othering as well as Belonging.

supremacy and the Othering of others. Just as family secrets were left dismembered from the corpus of us, so, too, the somatic, felt sense of the consequences of millennia of systemic Othering, structural racism, and extractive capitalism were shielded from my racialized and privileged white eyes. I am disappointed in myself for not seeing.

Of course, such unseeing, unknowing served me. It allowed me not to feel the pain of others. It allows me, and others who identify as I do, to move through the world wondering why "they" don't act like "us." Or to assert that, if "our" ancestors could make the transition from immigrant to white American, why can't "they."

And, of course, the "theys" are numerous; women in male-dominated boardrooms, Blacks in white-centered cultures, nonnative English speakers in rooms where there is no space for the multilingual and bicultural, where people of color are seen only through the lens of a stereotype.

When I was finally able to connect the dots between my childhood trauma and my adult bodily reflexes, it felt liberating.

But I can do better. I can endeavor to understand the somatic experiences of those around me.

Whether or not we see them, the disinherited are all around us. They are our neighbors, our friends, our family members, and, relevant to those of us who hold structural power and leadership positions, they are our colleagues. If our duty as leaders is to foster conditions of Belonging, then we must not only *see* them but strive to understand what life in their bodies is like; we must *feel* them.

Thinking back to my encounter with the woman whose ancestors were enslaved and brought to Haiti, I recall her challenge in asserting that she ought to be paid what her work deserved. I can imagine how her questioning her worthiness was so firmly held that it felt like a part of her nervous system. To her body, it was just a fact.

I'm thinking of Anne. A Black woman, Anne is a senior executive at a small company. She is enormously talented, and, as I often tell her, she lacks for nothing were she to choose to become a CEO.

Nothing, that is, but the self-confidence to assert what she knows to be true. One particular coaching session started off with a familiar routine. She was complaining about her boss not telling folks what he'd like, or where the company is going. "Just tell me what you want," she says to him all the time, "and I'll build it for you."

My body started squirming uncomfortably. It was as if my body were empathizing with her back against a wall, feeling her inability to embrace her strength, her own worthiness, her knowledge of what to do. I wanted so badly for her to take her seat as the leader I know she is.

Frustrated, I said, "The needle is stuck in the groove of the record." I was tired of it.

I said, "Anne, here we go again. You are deferring once more." In her organization's structure, she's the number two executive. And yes, she always waits for her CEO to tell the leadership team what to do. "He doesn't know what he wants," I said, exacerbated. "At least not beyond the six feet in front of him. Stop waiting for him."

Turning back to her presenting coaching agenda, to the reason she came to me for coaching, I said, "Look, I know this pattern is something we've worked on again and again. You come to the edge of something important and then pull yourself back to a safe place. But I want you to think of your ancestors."

I explained that the reunion process—and thinking of how it involves bringing up memories and reveries, and invoking the active imagination to step into the bodies of one's ancestors—allows us access their wisdom, to turn them into wise elders.

Imagining what they saw and what they smelled and what they experienced allows us to access their lives so that we may carry forward what they learned.

Moreover, why did they experience what they experienced if not to have their descendants, the fruition of their lives and labors, trials and tribulations, rise to take their seats as leaders.

She sat up straighter, taller. "What are they telling you right now?" I asked.

"They are reminding me that I know what I'm doing."

"What?" I asked, playfully trying to get her to repeat the line.

"I know what I'm doing!"

"And what does the company need from you?"

"I need to set the direction. I need to do what I keep asking my boss to do. I need to lead."

HOW MIGHT THE CONSEQUENCES OF OTHERING BE PRESENT IN YOUR BODY?

Speaking of the way the fear of the consequences of oppression become a "safety device" with which the oppressed, the disinherited, and the disposed surround themselves, Howard Thurman preached that doing so gives "some measure of protection from complete nervous collapse."

The disinherited do this, he says, by making "their bodies

commit to memory ways of behaving that will tend to reduce their exposure to violence."

This is happening all around us. These are our neighbors and friends. This is part of the daily experience of our colleagues and employees.

Through such bitter and constricted experiences, the disinherited have contorted their being to survive systemic Othering. To reduce the threat of danger, they have learned to be wary. Fearing the repercussions of a lineage of oppression, people will make themselves small in order to stay safe. Says Thurman, "Children are taught how to behave in this same way. The children of the disinherited live a restricted childhood."

As I write these words, the protest mantra "Hands up. Don't shoot" echoes in my head. I hear that and then I hear, again and again, "I can't breathe," the words of Eric Garner and George Floyd and far too many others.

Just as I didn't see the incarcerated, didn't think my writing was for them, didn't understand that they might resonate with my story, that their story *is* my story, I didn't see that the stories of the children of the disinherited are also my story.

Our obligation, our *religare* bond, is to see the disinherited and the restricted children of disinheritance through our everyday workplaces, our homes, and our communities.

Is their story any less deserving of being heard than your story?

THE LEAST OF THESE

I believe in the teachings of Jesus. I believe in the dharma of the Buddha. I want to be faithful to their words, and the meaning behind their words, especially when they spoke of "all be-ings" deserving love.

"'For I was hungry, and you gave me food, I was thirsty, and you gave me drink, I was a stranger and you welcomed me, I was naked, and you clothed me, I was sick, and you visited me, I was in prison, and you came to me.' Then the righteous will answer him, saying, 'Lord, when did we see you hungry and feed you, or thirsty and give you drink? And when did we see you a stranger and welcome you, or naked and clothe you? And when did we see you sick or in prison and visit you?' And the King will answer them, 'Truly, I say to you, as you did it to one of the least of these my brothers, you did it to me.'"*

I remember a moment on one of my trips to rural Tibet. Several of us were caravanning from one monastery to another. Our friends, monks from one of the monasteries, were riding shotgun, directing the drivers in our Toyota Land Cruisers. On a long, flat, concrete highway newly laid by the local government to cut hours off the travel time between villages, the monks asked us to stop. Looking down and ahead of the cars, they saw dozens of woolly caterpillars trying to cross the road. We stopped. The monks jumped out and gently picked up the caterpillars and helped them across. We waited for an hour until the road was clear of these woolly sentient beings.

Imagine if we treated all humans—the hungry, the sick, the children of the dispossessed and disinherited, the immigrants at our borders, those struggling to assert their self-worth after generations of internalized oppression, the imprisoned, the "least of these"—as these monks treated the caterpillars.

---

* Matthew 25:31–46.

The wisdom teachings of our elders are clear: All beings deserve love, safety, and, most importantly, Belonging.

I know it's hard. It's hard to open one's heart to a murderer or child abuser. It's hard for me as well. Indeed, it's harder for me to welcome into my heart one who has hurt a child than it is a murderer.

Working through my uncomfortable feelings about the incarcerated, I came to understand that my discomfort stemmed, partially, from the phenomenon of "your story is my story." Yes. There is a risk of falsely identifying with the Other, these disinherited.

But the greater risk is indifference. I do not want to join the fraternity of the indifferent. I do not want to look away. I do not want to be complicit in the dehumanization of another.

For guidance, I think of my teacher the American Buddhist nun Ani Pema Chödrön, and her relationship with Jarvis Masters, living his life on death row at San Quentin, and telling his story in books such as *Finding Freedom: How Death Row Broke and Opened My Heart.*

Holding space for, holding one's heart open to, the least of these demands a delicate, nuanced stance of not dismissing the consequences of their actions but seeing the larger forces at work and the ways they have been pawns in a great game of oppression, destruction, and Othering.

Against the great national myth of American exceptionalism is a disturbing reality of mass incarceration. We are, indeed, exceptional, but not in the ways we'd like to believe. We lock up a higher percentage of our population than any other economically privileged country.

This will always be so as long as we are complicit in, and benefit from, the dehumanization of others.

As I wrote earlier, dehumanization is a necessary condition for systemic Othering. This is true whether it's referring to a migrant on the southern border of the United States who's later bused from Texas to the vice president's house on Christmas Eve or my immigrant ancestor waiting anxiously for the right chalk mark on her lapel at Ellis Island. Dehumanization depends on those of us in power refusing to see the experience of our employees and their ancestors, much less those out of sight, waiting in detention centers or behind prison walls.

How can I call myself a leader if I ignore this reality, this dichotomy? I must hold both truths in my heart: murder is unconscionable, violence must be condemned, but truly seeing others and fostering deep, systemic Belonging make each of us, all of us, human.

THE CURRENCY CALLED COMPASSION

Of course, it's not only the incarcerated who live restricted lives.

Consider how many colleagues and friends live their lives reading and responding to spaces dominated by those from whom they differ.

Think about the woman who clutches her keys as she exits a subway and heads to her apartment, the keys like claws because of the epidemic of violence against women. Think of the young girl desperately counting the minutes as the pregnancy test runs through its analysis and tells her if she must somehow leave the state, find sanctuary, to get the healthcare she needs.

Or the Black lesbian who, once again, finds herself decolonizing white space, male space, straight space, having to field questions about diversity, equity, and inclusion because, of course, she should have the answers to a lack of justice in a space where others hold the power.

Think about, perhaps for the first time ever, the constancy of code-switching. Switching not just between spoken languages the way those who speak different languages do but as a survival strategy, a stratagem of Belonging designed to outwit, outlast, out endure systemic Othering. Imagine with your heart, and not just your mind, code-switching between body languages, between ways of being. Think of the Black man worrying that his language is too Black, his dress inappropriate, his dreadlocks simply wrong, somehow a threat to the white policeman who pulls him over because he's got an air freshener dangling from his rearview mirror.

Think of the woman who's been repeatedly warned that she is too much. Think of the man misgendered since birth, passing, hiding, code-switching his way over his true self, ever-cognizant of the epidemic of violence against transgender folks.

Think of the children of recent immigrants who carry the twin burdens of disconnection from a heritage culture or language as well as the burden of representation. Think of the Asian American child growing up with the expectation of being the good immigrant but who nevertheless stands in the doorway of the sorority party, questioning whether she belongs or if they, the others, think she got into that school only because the scales are tipped in favor of (or against) folks who look like her.

These are our family members. These are our friends. Look with widening eyes; these are our colleagues and employees. These and millions of others who live the restricted lives as children of disinheritance. These are our siblings who encounter the day-to-day instantiations of not Belonging and subjugation.

Psychologist Lisa Weisz-Lipton wrote of subjugation, the act of bringing another under one's control, from the vantage point of having been formerly incarcerated. Speaking of the corrections officers, the subjugators, who guarded her when she was incarcerated, she notes, "The roles had been defined for us, with decades of pop culture references and deeply engrained stereotypes reinforcing each other."

People assigned to the role of corrections officer internalized the notion that they had power *over* other people, while those in prison khakis, she notes, internalized the notion that others had power *over them*. They were helpless to effectuate change in their lives and needed to subjugate themselves to those who held power.

She witnessed this "power over" dynamic daily as she was constantly referred to as "inmate Lipton." She had reminded herself, she says, that it was only a construct, "not a reality."

Still, as professor john a. powell points out, constructs are a *form* of reality. Live long enough within a construct of *less than*, live long enough with your back against a wall and a knee or foot on your neck, and that construct becomes your reality. Substitute the words *settler, colonizer,* or even *members of a master race, a better class, a more-deserving caste,* and you can see how such constructs feed the power dynamics that pass for organization structures and community hierarchies.

Intellectually lazy but with self-reinforcing benefit to those with power over others, such hierarchies of the subjugated and the subjugators are the norm in our workplaces and communities.

The reunion process, with its call to do our first works over, demands that we reconsider traditional hierarchies and, importantly, all power dynamics. Reconsidering the effects of power allows us to imagine the possibility that lurking within the emphasis on productivity might be a latent reinforcement of supremacy, white or otherwise. A proper reunion can happen only when one peeks over the walls of separation and beyond subjugation and sees those imprisoned within these constructs. See them and listen to their stories.

Power-over dynamics, by furthering the effects of millennia of internalized oppression, maintain the walls of separateness and keep the Other unknown and, therefore, a threat.

Distorted, twisted, made small, those who identify from social locations outside of a heteronormative, binary-gender, white-male-dominant narrative pay the wages of this separation—physically, emotionally, economically, and existentially.

NEVER ENOUGH

The challenge of contorting oneself to avoid physical and existential violence can manifest in the persistent belief that one is never good enough. The persistent refrain of *never enough* can then lead to an internalized form of subjugation in which we all become "inmate Lipton." *Never enough* is a form of not being enough and, therefore, undeserving of fair compensation, equity, justice, love, safety, and, even, Belonging.

It's the persistent sense that I'm not enough so I can't do enough and therefore can't be enough . . . not only for love, safety, and Belonging but to make certain that I redeem my ancestors and don't let them fall out of the privileged classes.

It also feeds a pervasive imposter syndrome. And that syndrome can be particularly pronounced among the children of diaspora. Call it the immigrant's dilemma, but victims of pogroms and genocide, those of us who have lineages rife with famine and deprivation, are particularly susceptible to doubting our worthiness. Like the young Haitian woman at my book reading, *never enough* might be the root cause of believing oneself insufficient to demand appropriate compensation. For the disinherited and their children, *never enough* is the internalized oppression directly experienced by their ancestors, taken root in their bodies.

Part of the great myth of business leadership is that the power of *never enough* can be channeled and mastered into drive and motivation, traits so often seen as sacred to the pursuit of a goal. The myth is that we can cherry-pick the good known as motivation while leaving behind the devastating negative of *not good enough*.

I have a client, Patricia, who identifies as a white, straight woman. She was recently named the CEO of a venture capital–backed start-up that needed a bit of a turnaround. She'd left her previous job because she'd been passed over for a promotion—a promotion that, by all rights, should have gone to her—and took her seat for the first time as a CEO. We'd begun working shortly before she landed the new position, so I've been able to watch her as she slowly confronted her *never enough* subroutines.

One day she presented the perfect example of the behavior. Our call was on a Tuesday, and, as she explained when we started speaking, she'd spent most of the weekend rewriting the code behind the company's core offering.

"Patricia, what are you doing?" I asked. "You have thirty engineers and a head of engineering to do that work. Why are you reworking the software?"

As we unpacked her decision to do the work of others on her team, what emerged was a belief system—learned as a child longing to belong to her father, longing for the approval of a man who died too young—that, no matter how hard she worked (and Patricia works incredibly hard), nothing is good enough and so she must work even harder.

"It seems like whenever you're under duress, whenever you're stressed," I pointed out, "your learned response is to double down and work even harder, bypassing the opportunity to reexamine what and how you're doing things to see if there's a better, more scalable way."

I told her that gripping the wheel of leadership so tightly as to white-knuckle your way through is diametrically opposed to the real task of being a leader—to grow the team, to foster a sense of Belonging, and thereby to create more leaders within the team.

This white-knuckling *never enough* drive hurts. Sometimes *never enough*, springing from the leader's need for more and more, becomes embedded in a company's culture and all feel it satisfied only by the hungry ghost desire for more—more customers, more growth, more profit.

Indeed, for the team, *never enough* leads to a reliance on doing and urgency, both sensibilities supporting the persistent and systemic Othering.

Urgency, speediness, and, for many organizations, the persistent need to "scale" for no discernible reason, other than the presumption that bigger is better, is unchecked extractive capitalism. This stands in opposition to the need and respect for rest and recovery. It also fosters a view of the self that highlights productivity and rational, objective results even as it strips away the humanity of a community of co-workers, wildflowers all, undermining any semblance of systemic Belonging.

RADICAL INDIVIDUALISM

The Western self, says john a. powell, is isolated and separate. For millennia, the history of the self is a fabrication, a conjunction with ideals that assert a "radical individualism." These ideals include a hyperrationality, the primacy of objectivity, market capitalism, and, where it's been useful, the construction of race. "This notion of the self," he writes in *Racing to Justice*, "is at the core of the American dream of liberty and opportunity for all, of pure meritocracy." But equally important, it also leads to exclusion and domination. Exclusion, meaning division and those familiar walls of separateness, and domination, as in the subjugation that comes from the *power over* dynamic.

One way this manifests is the problematic notion of meritocracy—a concept as central to the American ideal as exceptionalism. The leaders of many Silicon Valley companies extoll the virtues of meritocracy, once again cherry-picking the good while ignoring the negative effect. When so many have grown into adulthood in the absence of true equity, it's impossible to ascertain merit without considering justice.

I like to see myself, for example, as having pulled myself up from the poverty of my childhood by my own bootstraps. It is a useful image that reinforces my self-confidence. But when I'm honest with myself, I admit that it's hard to know the effect of my whiteness on whatever success I've achieved.

A seminal moment in my life, for example, was when a

favorite professor awarded me a scholarship that covered the cost of my tuition for the last two years of my time in college. While part of me knows that Dr. Greenberg saw and rewarded my merit, part of me also knows that he may have seen kinship in our stories—both sets of our ancestors migrated from Europe, from nonwhite to white. And that kinship may have made him more likely to see the merit in me instead of the merit in a classmate racialized as nonwhite.

This is one reason why the primacy of meritocracy is problematic. Building organizations that are centered on a problematic notion potentially undermines systemic Belonging. Therefore, reward and advancement based on merit require discernment and the type of radical inquiry I promote for all leaders who strive to be better humans. Mindsets, like the fixation on merit, too often and conveniently overlook the consequences of internalized oppression, lineages of systemic trauma, or systemic Othering through exclusion and domination.

For someone who prided himself on having pulled himself out of a challenging past, for someone who took great comfort in Carl Jung's declaration "I am not what has happened to me, I am what I choose to become," it's central to my identity to consider my own agency in overcoming adversity.

Part of my reunion process, however, has been coming to terms with this duality. Both of these statements are true: I worked hard to overcome my past, and I was helped along the way by the privilege afforded me by my ancestors' journey to whiteness.

As challenging as that notion was for me to accept, it was also liberating. Letting go of meritocracy, like letting go of patriarchy and, even, supremacy, meant also letting go of the myth of rugged, hyper-individualism. Seeing the limits of meritocracy means reuniting with the fierce reality of my life and the lives around me.

It means letting go of the primacy of the leader as the strong man, responsible for all the good (and, concomitantly, the bad) of any endeavor. When we release ourselves from the notion of the leader as strong man, leading by dint of the maximum merit and with a radical individualism, we allow the rest of the team to take their seats as adults, as equals, in the organization. We also create more possibility and potentially more equity for the disinherited because we move away from exclusion, subjugation, and domination.

We also limit erasure. This erasure, this willful not seeing of others, leads to not caring, the loss of compassion. One is reminded of Hannah Arendt's observations about the banality of evil—not seeing, not caring, leads to the logical consequence of silence.

The primacy of objective rationality as well of the myth of meritocracy end up supporting the evil that is white supremacy and patriarchy.

How comfortable are you with seeing the effects of privilege in your life? Both the benefits and, too, the complicity in the system that maintain Othering?

As a white, straight, cisgender man, I had to teach myself to see the limits of objective rationality and the mythic nature of meritocracy. I had to give up a view of myself that was precious to my identity.

What would you lose if you were to see the often unseen and unnamed forces that have both held you *back* as well as, importantly, held you *up?*

LIVING AS SIBLINGS OR PERISHING AS FOOLS

Writing in his introduction to *The Radical King*, Dr. Cornel West notes that Dr. King believed that indifference to evil is greater than evil itself. This indifference, plus the materialism of extractive capitalism upon which it is based, "produces sleepwalkers bereft of compassion and zombies deficient in love."

He notes that this spiritual crisis is rooted in the decline of integrity, honesty, decency, and virtue—all foreseeable consequences of father-hungry, elder-less, hungry ghost leaders holding power over others. It also results in a "coldhearted obsession with manipulation and domination" that creates toxicity in our communities and our companies.

Moral consistency, systemic analyses, critical thinking that encourages questioning of the gauzy origin myths are precisely what the radical individualist fear most. In Buddhism we're taught about the power of prajna: discerning wisdom that cuts like a flaming sword through delusion. We need the critical flaming sword of analysis to cut through the myths— the lies—that prevent us from seeing and feeling the effects of Othering on our brothers and sisters. Reunion is, in some sense, a profound expression of our interdependence.

Indifference, too, perpetuates the evil of erasure, and the death coming from silence. In his essay "The Violence of Desperate Men," Martin Luther King Jr. warned that "noncooperation with evil is just as much a moral duty as is cooperation with good." Looking away, as well as systemically refusing to see erasure, existential violence, subjugation, and systemic Othering, is cooperation with evil.

Do you see the lives of the disinherited? They work right

next to you. The denial of our own stories becomes an imped-
iment to seeing the stories of those around us, including the
disinherited and their children. If they are not seen, how can
they feel they belong?

Dr. King noted that one of the great disappointments of
human history is that too many of us fail to remain awake
through periods of great social change. Every society, he says,
has its "protectors of the status quo" and their "fraternities of
the indifferent" who sleepwalk through revolutions. The great
reunion depends upon our waking up and staying awake.
"The large house in which we live demands that we transform
this worldwide neighborhood into a worldwide brotherhood,"
wrote Dr. King in "The World House." "We must learn to live
as brothers or together perish as fools."

When CEOs refuse to take a stand against evil, they refuse to heed the longings of their employees to work for and
live in a world where they feel they belong. Better leaders are
not just better humans, they reject indifference.

The Tibetan Buddhist teacher Chögyam Trungpa used to
bless people with a wish: "May you be bombarded with co-
conuts of wakefulness." Every time I hear someone being accused of being woke, I think of that wish. Overcoming knees
on necks, breaching the ramparts of separation, demands that
we wake up, and remain awake, to this moment of possibility,
this moment of potential great social change. We cannot sleep
through this revolution. There are, as Jackson Browne once
sang, lives in the balance. There are people under fire and
children at the cannons.

Seeing the hearts, minds, and bodies of the disinherited requires an empathetic imagination. One of the gifts of the reunion process is that it fires the empathetic imagination. When

we take the time to step into the Othered bodies of our ancestors, for example, it opens the possibility of our stepping into the somatic experiences of all the disinherited.

Just as we must when we endeavor to coach someone, just as we ought to when we are called to lead, we listen and observe with curiosity, tapping into our own experiences for relevant information about how something might feel for the other. We take extreme care to avoid presumptions and assumptions about the other's experiences (and keeping clear of our tendency to fix and, therefore, negate the agency of the other). We are called upon to imagine what it is like to step into their bodies and to understand viscerally their experiences. This is how we visit those in prison, as Jesus counseled; this is how we hear their stories.

This, to my mind and heart, is the essence of *religare*, keeping the bond—remembering, and therefore beginning the process of repairing that which has been severed. Such is the essence of leadership. Such is the essence of the reunion process.

Each of us lives in two realms, noted King. The internal realm is spiritual, the place of the *religare*; it is often expressed in art, morals, and the beauty of a well-crafted sentence. The external is a complex of mechanisms and the outcomes and outputs of our actions. The external real is where we engage beyond shaking our head at mass incarceration and knees on necks, and move into action, taking stands against banal evil. It is how we lead. It is how we live.

The *religare*, meeting the obligation of our bond with the divine as well with each other, fosters systemic Belonging in our societies. Leadership for the disinherited, for those with backs against the wall . . . hell, for each of us, regardless of our privilege or lack of it, requires a balancing of the inner and outer.

The greater our material wealth, the greater the peril if it's not accompanied by a proportionate growth of the soul. Warned King: "When the external of man's nature subjugates the internal, dark storm clouds begin to form." When wealth becomes power for either the individual or a nation, the disinherited and the wretched of the earth are left to fend for themselves in the storm that is life.

Such is the dilemma of modern corporate leadership with its focus on enlarging material powers and maintaining stock prices while extracting more and more from the land and from people. Such an emphasis, based as it is on the separation of the inner and outer realms, impedes any systemic attempts to create Belonging. Such a separation not only breaks the bond with the divine but severs any chance for the reconciliation and repair.

REMEMBER AND REPAIR

Just as we need to "do our first works over" to repair what has been broken, repairing the effects of systemic Othering to lay the foundation for systemic Belonging requires that leaders do our work.

Leaders and others who hold power have a moral responsibility to tell the truth.

And the truth cannot be told until those who hold power reunite and remember.

As I consider what is necessary to foster systems of Belonging in our organization, I gather the steps. I do this for myself as much as for you—well-intentioned leaders with power and privilege who, like me, want to move beyond tsk-tsking our responses to structural racism and systemic Othering and do our first works over.

Moving forward, author Lisa Sharon Harper notes, "requires us to understand the depth of our brokenness." It also demands, she says, that we reckon with the reality that our current structures have been tainted by hundreds of years of policy set up to favor people of European descent at the expense of all others. Understand this and accept that by *not* acknowledging it, we unconsciously maintain these systems and structures.

For descendants of European immigrants, for those racialized as white, we must also remember the epigenetic, intergenerational memory and trauma of having been Othered, for it was that experience that led to a fierce resolve to see the Other as a threat.

To do this, writes Rhonda Magee in *The Inner Work of Racial Justice*, we need to commit to work every day to minimize oppression, to be an active co-conspirator. Magee adds: "We need the will to repair the many separations that characterize the sense we have of ourselves as individuals apart from one another, and distinct from the air we breathe and the earth to which we will all one day return."

PERMISSION TO BE OURSELVES

See the disinherited. Listen to them. Step into their place and imagine the stories held in their bodies. Do not *take* their story, do not appropriate it, but *relate* to it, acknowledging the differences in our experiences all while listening somatically and with curiosity. Pay attention to your own body as they describe, for example, what may have happened to them or how it feels in their body.

By asking ourselves what it feels like in our bodies, we open to the possibility of the empathetic *religare*, the essential reunion. As you hear their stories, stay present. Notice, but don't give in to, your desire to defend or explain. Notice any wish to equate, hiding behind a stated desire to relate. Stay curious.

What might the other's experience of being Othered be like in their body? Imagine what it is to be them. Listen to their words.

I often share the experience of being asked to help organizations where trust is broken. I'll typically start by asking folks if they've been telling each other the truth.

"The truth?" they'll respond, shocked. "Oh, no, we don't trust each other to tell the truth."

In organizations where systemic Othering is the norm, it's usually unsafe to tell the truth. And the clearest tell that it's unsafe to share the truth of the lived experiences is the inability of those in power to listen.

Without trust, there is no safety. Without safety, there is no Belonging. And without listening, there is no trust.

Listen and see the inter-beingness in that which may be shared or similar but do not take their stories as your own. Know that our stories remain separate, even as they remain a bridge of the separation and division.

Such deep listening requires patience.

Listening to create safety and trust as foundational components of systemic Belonging will ask much of leaders. It will be especially challenging for those who measure their own self-worth by speediness, external accomplishments, an anxiety-fueled urgency, or rising valuations. Listening for Belonging requires the ability to wait patiently for the whole answer to reveal itself. Listening for Belonging requires the patience to sometimes hear the same answer again and again until the tears, the pain, the fears have run their course.

These are knee-on-the-neck, backs-against-the-wall, lives-in-the-balance, take-it-to-the-streets times. We must understand the wages of separation. We must ask again and again, with the same patience and fortitude we are to give others, how we have been complicit in, and benefited from, the systemic Othering we say we do not want.

If not, our children will continue to face down pepper sprays and out-of-control viruses as others of our children are shot in their beds after no-knock warrants.

CHAPTER 7

The Longing to Belong

It is not your duty to finish the work, but neither are you
at liberty to neglect it.
—RABBI TARFON*

That the work need not be finished is as liberating as the
notion that it can't be neglected is daunting. While we are
liberated from the burden of completion, we are challenged by
the command to do the work. We must work regardless of the
outcome.

In this way, the work of Belonging can seem Sisyphean.
We roll the boulder up the hill so that the disinherited, dispossessed, and, indeed, all whom we are privileged to lead,
may feel loved, safe, and that they belong, only to confront
the hidden reality of mass incarceration and deaths by overpolicing in our communities. We hear the anguish of those
disinherited of their human rights by laws that restrict a
woman's right to choose her own healthcare. We dutifully
attend corporate programs to surface unconscious bias and,
if we are lucky, discover that, as in so many aspects of our

---

*   Pirkei Avot 2: 21.

life, we who hold power have been complicit in maintaining the conditions we say we don't want. We have benefited from systems of oppression which we steadfastly claim we loathe.

We come to accept that one of the not-to-be-neglected tasks is to confront with loving curiosity what it is that we might be willing to give up—the safety that comes from our racialized identity, for example—in order that another might feel the safety of Belonging.

We muscle up that boulder in our well-intentioned efforts to participate in the creation of systems that value people over profit only to be dinged by investors for our quixotic dreams of beloved community. Our company's share price plunges, and our job as CEO is threatened, because we've given our employees a little more time off to parent and love their children. We adopt environmental, social, and governance (ESG) standards designed to build companies that contribute meaningfully to a better world for our colleagues, for our children, only to be attacked. We're told that these ESG goals are little more than a covert drive for a progressive agenda through economic coercion and an ignoring of democratic processes. The will and the choice of investors and stockholders—those privileged to have the economic means to participate in an economic uplifting of the few over the safety of the many—have had their economic rights trampled merely because we've sacrificed a little profit to minimize the damage to people and the planet.

In the Sisyphean bind, we may fail to comprehend that all this is distraction. Such critics wish that we would ignore the wages of separation so that they may continue to feel the safety their ancestors won for them. We might tsk-tsk and console ourselves with, "Well, I tried."

But, as the rabbi taught, we are not allowed to neglect the work. We are not allowed to say with resignation, "Well, I tried."

For years, I've asked clients to frame their work, work they must do even though it might never be finished, as a call to build companies that they would like to work for. "Build organizations," I'd counsel, "where you would be proud if your children worked there."

Such companies, I assert, are not merely defined by purpose, ethical values, and a persistent sense of Belonging but are sustainably strong. Such companies are healthy containers in which Belonging, ethics, and purpose become the content that gives shape and meaning to the container. Belonging, and not wealth creation for investors, becomes the purpose of building healthy, profitable containers.

The work that is not our duty to finish but remains our duty to undertake, then, is the work of creating businesses that are meaningful, content-rich containers where the longing to belong is recognized, celebrated, and, faithfully, answered. The dutiful never-ending work, then, is reunion, the process that not only counters Othering but reunites each of us with the innate sense of Belonging that is our birthright. The liberating, never-needing-to-be-finished work that is our duty to undertake and keep undertaking is embodied in the reunion process and results in communities and companies that are safe, loving, houses of Belonging for all, including and especially for the children of disinheritance.

COMPANIES WORTHY OF THE WORK

One of my clients identifies as a Chinese American woman. She is cisgender and straight. A CEO, her dedication to building a successful and inclusive culture is profoundly held. Indeed, nearly every conversation we have circles back to the ways she holds herself to living up to her own standards of inclusivity. Having spent so much of her career on the periphery of white, male-dominated leadership circles, she knows the somatic and emotional wages of striving while living on the margins.

I surprised her when we began working together by suggesting that her first act in becoming the CEO she was born to be was to take up the work of radical self-inquiry. That as well as her own reunion process. I asked her to envision not merely her parents but her grandparents and, stretching the bounds of her knowledge, her great-grandparents.

I did this because her identity as a woman in a male-dominated field is critical to her notion of who she wants to be as a CEO. I asked her about the women of her lineage because I wanted her to see the ways her ancestors' wishes, dreams, fears, and experiences have already shaped how she leads. I did this so that we could access those elders.

"My great-grandmother's family came from the upper classes in China," she told me after researching a bit. As was customary for her family's social class, her great-grandmother's father had several wives and dozens of children. Status and Belonging even within the family were tenuous and, in many cases, limited by gender. Caste and gender occasionally determined who lived past birth.

For the girls who were allowed to grow into women, there

could be bone-breaking wages to pay. My client continued, "And my great-grandmother's feet were bound so tightly that she couldn't walk."

The fact of her great-grandmother having to be carried made me think of how another client's mother would describe *her* Chinese mother, whose feet were also bound: "An exquisite, perfect doll," whose nobility was preserved with broad-brimmed hats ensuring her "porcelain skin" remained a hallmark of her upper-class status. Such women were worshipped and preserved as delicate objects while their very human existence was denied. Broken bones hidden under silk wraps and porcelain skin.

We paused to grieve. We imagined the silk-wrapped broken bones of her ancestor. We remembered that which was dismembered, glossed over as simply another family story from the Old World. The memory of the wage of separation paid by Great-grandma was severed from the family consciousness. Her descendants had buried the memory under the horrors of a civil war that split a society and caused Great-grandma's descendants to move toward the perceived safety of, first, Taiwan and then, later, America, where their labors were welcome but their bodies not so much.

"Asian Americans inhabit a vague purgatorial status," writes poet Cathy Park Hong in her collection of essays *Minor Feelings*. Neither white nor Black enough, distrusted by Black Americans and ignored by whites unless they were being used to keep other nonwhite folks down, she adds, "We are the carpenter ants of the service industry, the apparatchiks of the corporate world. We are math-crunching middle managers who keep the corporate wheels greased but who never get promoted since we don't have the right 'face' for leadership."

Passive, impassive, and perhaps even porcelain, frantically overcompensating to hide devouring feelings of inadequacy, she describes her community. The literature regarding self-hatred among members of communities outside the dominant supremacist culture is helpful, provocative, and thoughtful but, as Hong notes, limited; not enough, for example, has been said about self-hatred and internalized oppression among Asian Americans. "Racial self-hatred," Hong writes, "is seeing yourself the way the whites see you, which turns you into your own worst enemy."

The image of impassive worker ants dutifully supporting the mechanisms of the corporate structure fresh in our minds, I asked my client, "What might your frantic efforts to succeed be in service to?"

And further, "Why is it so important to create equity and inclusivity? What's behind that drive?" I let the questions hang in the air a bit; they morphed into a rhetorical observation. "For whom might you be working to realize this potential?"

After the memories of the women in her lineage were brought forth, after she reunited with her own bone-breaking and complex binds—for example, to fully represent the voices of those outside the dominant structure of race and gender while constrained by the demands of how whites might see her—we had a clearer understanding of her leadership journey: meeting the longing for Belonging. Both hers as well as that of those whom she's been tasked to lead.

As part of her process of building the company she'd like to work for, one in which all might fully belong, she remembered the unsaid facts and not merely the gauzy myths of her ancestors. Together we continued to explore the known as well as the unsaid, secret facts of her lineage and, most importantly, how those no-longer-secret facts influence her everyday decisions.

In exploring such unasked questions, in saying out loud the unsaid facts of her family, she sought the strength dormant in her great-grandmother's body. Strength, and a personal connection to the purpose of Belonging that is far deeper than an intellectualized commitment to ethics. *Belonging is the point of her leadership.*

For her first step in building the company she wants to work for, the first step in fostering an empathy so sorely lacking, was to understand her own stories. And with such understanding came the ability to hear and relate to the other's story. She was better able to navigate the complex intersectional challenges—challenges of race, gender identity, classism, and other forms of potential Othering—that come with building diverse and inclusive companies.

By knowing her own story, by using radical self-inquiry to look beyond even her own complicity in creating the conditions of her life but into the curious lineage of her ancestors, she has become even more empathetic. She might hear the stories of those whom she is privileged to lead. In a second step in her reunion journey, she turned her radical self-inquiry into a curiosity about others, thereby opening to the possibility of "your story is my story."

"Your story is my story" is the foundational component of systemic Belonging precisely because it fosters empathy, knowing, and connection regardless of power dynamics. Doing this work doesn't guarantee success, but neglecting the work guarantees failure.

LEADERSHIP AND THE FORCES OF OTHERING

What's needed is nothing short of a transformation of the traditional notion of leadership. It is no longer sufficient to measure success by financial return on investment, for example. Good leaders must also use the experience of leadership to confront demons. They must encounter and understand the subroutines that define their lives and see the ways such inherited belief systems shape the positive and negative experiences of those whom they are called to lead.

To do this work will mean understanding and, often, reframing the messages from our ancestors. Doing so turns such ghostly ancestors into wise elders.

The next phase of this work, however, is outer focused. Those of us who hold power must use the same tools of inquiry to reframe the society-wide subroutines that conspire to maintain oppression in the mistaken belief that it is necessary to our safety. Neglecting this work maintains the systems of Othering that oppressed our ancestors as well as our brothers and sisters across our communities. Indeed, neglecting this work furthers toxicity for those whom we lead. Modern leaders, leaders of companies that the world needs now, use reunion to actively confront Othering wherever it sprouts, including from their own inner demons.

One of the challenges, of course, is that their inner demons often collude with external demonic forces. Our self-doubt dances with the messages that our commitment to a healthy physical and social environment is somehow evidence of our imposter status as leaders. Such messages tell us that a leader's only responsibility is to do what it takes to create the highest economic return on investment. Indeed, the mantra we each receive is seductively simple: maximize shareholder return.

While it is true that, as I often say, it is a responsibility of business leaders to take a dollar and turn it into two, it is not their *only* responsibility. If it were, then we could say that those who grew fortunes by selling illegal drugs, creating Ponzi schemes, or otherwise violating basic notions of human decency are our most successful leaders. The logic behind the maximization of profit regardless of the cost, regardless of the wages of separation to be paid, has no end. Or, if you prefer, no bottom.

The real challenge is to build profitable containers where the content of the business is worthwhile, humane, and life-giving.

That inspirational challenge is too often and too conveniently ignored. The self-appointed anti-wokeness brigade is little different from the fraternities of the indifferent, identified long ago by Martin Luther King Jr. They are the guardians of a dystopian and self-annihilating pursuit of profit over all else. They fail to understand the logical conclusion of their winner-take-all, my-Belonging-at-the-cost-of-your-Belonging mindset is authoritarianism. It will not be software that eats the world, to paraphrase a famous venture capitalist, but a lack of empathy and compassion that will devour us all.

One of the essential responsibilities of power is to see the ways our individual struggles, the challenges of the individual fingers on the hand, can become the currency of compassion drawing us together. But this can happen only if we use this currency to buy the treasures of love, safety, and Belonging not merely for ourselves but for those we purport to lead.

The forces that maintain systemic Othering are relentless.

The forces that challenge Belonging in our workplaces, like the forces that challenge our love and safety in society at large, won't ever rest. We need leaders who can be co-conspirators in standing up for what is right.

Lacking leadership in our communities, lacking the ability to explore these issues in our schools (where teaching the history of racism in the United States is twisted and distorted and presented as "anti-white"), employees are yearning for answers. They are looking to those of us with power to model the confrontation with uncomfortable truths. They are looking to us for leadership.

Our children, our employees, our neighbors, and our friends are waiting for us to use our power to create the systemic changes we say we want to have in the world. They are waiting for us to use our privilege to actively conspire to create a world where our ancestors would be welcome.

Our silence undermines our leadership. Moreover, silence from us well-meaning, well-intentioned members of the dominant classes is no longer acceptable. We must speak up. We must take sides. Neutrality and neglecting the work that is to be done, taught the wise elder Elie Wiesel, help only the oppressor.

The people you lead, the employees of the companies you build, want to know that you care enough to take a side, to stand for something, that the container of the business has a purpose beyond the four walls of the company. That all of our labors add up to something even if it's quixotic.

A Talmudic handbook of Belonging would assert that when the inner work of understanding the journey of our own Belonging is not matched with the outer work of clearly seeing the ways we have maintained systemic oppression, the result will be less than humane, perhaps even inhumane, leadership.

The work that we may not neglect, the work that we are likely not to see end, begins with listening. Listening to ourselves by examining our beliefs, listening to ancestors so that we may learn the roots of those beliefs, and listening to others so that we may hear their stories and see the shared experiences of suffering.

WHAT'S A HEAVEN FOR?

I write this morning in the deepening shade of the monument to Cervantes on the Plaza de España in Madrid. Don Quixote sits astride Rocinante, while Sancho Panza is slightly to his left, to his rear.

I suppose my strident calls for a new definition of leadership may be quixotic. But as I traversed my own journey, from encounters with the ghosts of my ancestors and the secrets they held through to the battles and protests marking these times, I can see no other way through the pain of systemic Othering. More importantly, though, I see no better use for the privileges I have been given.

My mother loved Broadway musicals. Some of my most moving memories are of the Sunday afternoons when we didn't go to one or the other of my grandparents' homes for dinner but, instead, listened to music on our old hi-fi. Mom would take a scratchy vinyl disc from a battered and worn cardboard sleeve and put it on the record player covered in faux-wood plastic. When the records were to be played, the turntable flipped out and down.

Man of La Mancha was my favorite show. I didn't quite

understand this musical version of Don Quixote, but as a nerdy, sentimental kid, I loved the song "The Impossible Dream." With the black vinyl spinning, I'd lie on the worn carpet of our living room, silently singing along. I'd get chills midway through the song, "To right the unrightable wrong . . . / To try when your arms are too weary . . . / No matter how hopeless / No matter how far."

I'm probably naive. I may be quixotic, but I still dream of such things. "A man's reach should exceed his grasp," wrote Robert Browning. "Or what's a heaven for?" Being quixotic, reaching for the heaven that exceeds my grasp, feels right.

If those who hold power—by dint of their bodies, wealth, or normative cultural traditions of the societies in which they live—do not dedicate their leadership to the journey to systemic Belonging, then we will fail to live up to the responsibility of power and the promise of our humanity.

Such is the work of those with privileged inheritances. Such is the work of those who seek to understand the ways we have been complicit in, and benefited from, that which disinherits others.

There's a stinging *New Yorker* cartoon that occasionally makes it way as a meme. It stings because it's true. An adult sits at a campfire surrounded by a few kids. All are dressed in rags, signaling a dystopian future. The adult is speaking, "Yes, the planet got destroyed. But for a beautiful moment in time, we created a lot of value for shareholders."

We who hold power are in just such a moment. We have a choice. What are we willing to give up that we love in order to create systemic Belonging? How will we answer that question when we sit around the campfire with our descendants?

The task for a leader is to use our agency, our power, to feel our way to what is needed most. Think of the power of radical self-inquiry tools not merely as a means to understanding your complicity in the conditions of your life but as a mechanism for understanding what will be best at fostering systemic Belonging.

Once we fully understand who we are, how we got to be the person we are, and, most importantly, what we're really feeling, we get to expand our empathetic awareness of the other by listening somatically.

Sometimes, as a coach, I'll hear a client's words and they don't match the feelings in my body. "I'm fine," they'll say, as I notice a tension rising in my back or a queasiness in my stomach. Without detracting from the validity of their statements, I will use the experience in my body to get curious about what might be happening for my client. And sometimes, in these magical moments, my body will give expression to something the client is unaware of. Sometimes I trust my intuition, enhanced by somatic awareness, and ask the right question that unlocks a deeper, generative learning. In those moments, we both grow.

Now imagine the felt sense of inclusion that would accompany the experience where those in power listened as much with their heart (and their bodies) as with their heads.

When we listen with our heart, we hear the longing for Belonging in others. When we listen with the heart and drop our need to fix, we bear witness to their story. Being witnessed, especially nonjudgmentally and especially by those who have power, strengthens safety—that essential pillar of Belonging.

Early on my own path to understanding my need for safety and Belonging, I built on the guidance of my then psychoanalyst, Dr. Avivah Sayres. She'd encourage me to ask myself essential questions such as, What am I not saying that I need to say?

Later, as I internalized the radical self-inquiry I had learned in analysis into my work as a leader and a coach, I expanded on that question by further inquiring into what it was that I might be saying that wasn't being heard. More relevant, though, I used that process to create safety for others by seeking to understand what it was that was being said that I was not hearing—because I was too busy tapping my watch and not listening enough with my heart.

What am I saying that's not being heard? and What's being said that I'm not hearing? are two essential questions that can foster the conditions of listening for the longing to belong.

In the work of writing *Reunion*, though, I had to expand my inquiry into what was being said that I wasn't hearing. When I first inquired into that question, I unconsciously looked away from the way my own privilege, my own whiteness, and even my own internalized racism and misogyny contributed to my not hearing that which was being said. In a patriarchal, white supremacist society that values linear productivity over difference, in a world where difference is threatening, we are too often reared to shut out diverse voices.

The literature of leadership, for example, too often lacks voices outside the white, heteronormative, and colonizer mindset. (Lest I go further, I must acknowledge with irony that I am a white, straight, cisgender man who has been given the privilege of a platform by speaking and writing books.)

We must read voices outside the bubbles of our experiences. And we share the microphone with those whom the dominant culture has excluded from the dialogue. Exclusion from the dialogue also often means exclusion from leadership, exclusion from equitable power sharing. I can only imagine how exhausting it is to confront these seemingly impenetrable barriers.

"Patiently educating a clueless white person about race is draining," says Cathy Park Hong. "It takes all your powers of persuasion. Because it's more than a chat about race. It's ontological. It's like explaining to a person why you exist, or why you feel pain, or why your reality is distinct from their reality."

Those of us privileged with power must hear what is being said. We must listen to hear the longing, the pain, and the distinct realities. Once again, imagine a world in which those in power were able to listen with empathy to someone who, say, identifies as a woman repeatedly asserting that they have a right to exist, have feelings and rights to self-determination. Imagine identifying as nonbinary and having, yet again, to justify your preferred pronouns to someone made mildly uncomfortable by what they perceive to be awkward grammar. To do otherwise is to tap an annihilating watch.

What I'm essentially calling for is a form of listening that is based completely in empathy and not primarily in output or problem-solving.

This is what our employees are yearning for. Recall that the dominant complaint about leaders, gleaned from studying hundreds of performance reviews, is the lack of empathy by those in power.

If the wish to foster Belonging isn't motivation enough, consider this fact: the most likely cause of a leader's failure is their inability to read and meet the needs of their employees, to heed their longing to belong. You can ignore the strident calls from folks like me but look at the data. When your employees want you to take a stand for Black Lives Matter, for instance, they want you to lead with your heart, with empathy. They want you to give a shit.

Be warned. Expanding the definition of successful leadership to include having a heart that is filled with compassion, that cares about a world in which fourth graders and innocent Black men are murdered, in which gender-questioning children and adult women are denied healthcare, causes a reckoning not only with the systems of oppression with which you may have benefited. It will cause a reckoning with your own sense of self. It will cause you to do your work.

DOING YOUR WORK AS A LEADER

Many years ago, to summarize my work as a leadership coach, I created a graphic with which I could quickly communicate what it was that I believed was necessary for those with power to lead well and live with equanimity.

Practical Skills + Radical Self-Inquiry + Shared Experiences
Enhanced Leadership + Greater Equanimity

Now, after this journey of reuniting with past and, through them, present experiences of so many of my friends, family members, and colleagues, I would alter that formula. The newer, updated formula provides a path for the work of a leader worthy of the term. It considers the outer experience of those of us who would lead as well as the lived experiences of those whom we have the honor and duty to serve.

Practical Skills + (Radical Self-Inquiry + Reunion) + Shared Experiences
_____
Enhanced Leadership + Greater Equanimity + Systemic Belonging

To live up to the promise of this revised formula, I must recommit daily to do my work, to reunite, to tear down the walls of separation, to earn the admiration of my descendants, and to heed the longing to belong all around me.

REMEMBERING THAT WHICH WAS DISMEMBERED

"We know ourselves," wrote poet and student of Buddhism bell hooks, "through the art and act of remembering." And the Buddhist teacher Pema Chödrön sees remembering as an act of welcoming the unwelcome.

This "art and act" of entering the room called Remember is, then, a commitment to reunite with the forgotten, secret, unspoken, and unwelcome parts of our stories. It is, therefore, an essential part of the reunion process, of answering one's own longing to belong.

But like so many other experiences fostered and supported by radical self-inquiry, it turns out to be essential to answering the longing of others. Motivated perhaps by alleviating one's own suffering, we enter the room called Remember. The essential first step is radical self-inquiry that leads to a whole self, which clears the path for the vital second step: the reunification with the other through the art and act of seeing the other's story in our own story. In doing so, we do the work that need not be completed but may not be neglected. In doing so, we embark on the work that binds us first to ourselves and then to one another.

For the art and act of welcoming the unwelcome clears our toxic patterns, enabling us to use the power of our positions to call forth systemic Belonging—even during the most trying times, especially during the most trying times.

GOING FIRST

It's not obvious but it's true that going first is a form of truth telling. When those who hold power in any community share their story with the genuine attempt to say the unsaid, unwelcome things, we not only create possibility of the connection implicit in "your story is my story" but we foster a safety that may make it possible for those with less power to share their stories.

I think of Charles, a friend who, like my client, had ancestors that were wealthy landowners in the Commonwealth of Virginia. Their roots stretch back to when the land was the colony of Virginia. Of course, that land was taken from Indigenous folks and, of course, that land was worked by enslaved people. While not as clear as the connections in Jamie's past, Charles still struggles to understand his relationship to power. Therefore, so does the small firm he leads. Time and again, on walks in the hills not far from my home, we speak about the inchoate yet ever-present discomforts in the team.

I leave our walks wondering what would happen if my friend went first and told the truth of the benefits that came to him by the slavery that benefited his family.

Perhaps, too, the lies and secrets that surround his brother's addictions and depressions—more things unsaid, unnamed in the secret-keeping family culture—might be released and thereby relieved, not unconsciously forced to be relived. Telling the truth is often about taking sides. Taking sides in the way elder Elie Wiesel would have us do.

Companies can struggle with telling the truth. As I've shared, I'll often joke while pointing out the ways avoiding truth—and, if you will, conflict—undermines trust and, therefore, innovation. But relevant to this discussion, avoiding the truth undermines Belonging at every turn.

It is true, for example, that we in the United States have a problem with overpolicing and that it is related to a history of mass incarceration. It is also true that these problems support white supremacy. For any progress to be made on each of these issues, we must start with what is true.

More prosaically, and connecting to our organizations, good leaders who tell and welcome the truth foster the Belonging that comes from clear feedback. To be able to give clear, unambiguous feedback to those in power is also an act of truth telling. In his wonderful blessing "For a Leader," poet John O'Donohue urges leaders be surrounded by good friends who "mirror your blind spots." Indeed, he further notes that when someone fails us, may the graciousness with which we meet them be their "stairway to renewal and refinement."

In this way, creating cultures of "going first" and truth becomes even more than an act of renewal. It becomes the ground for reconciliation and, ultimately, redemption. Truth may lead to regret, something that can feel painful. But we must remember that regret may lead to reconciliation, and reconciliation is the basis of all reunion. Reunion—both internal and external—creates the possibility of reparation, repair, and, ultimately, redemption for the wages of separation.

REDEMPTION

Redemption, then, is at the core of Belonging. For example, organizations that prize truth-based regret, renewal, and refinement—essential steps implicit in the promise of redemption—center the art and act of their values and actions around reparation and the restoration of the natural states of justice and compassion. Systemic Belonging becomes a consequence of systemic redemption, for it is the act of renewal that reinforces safety—safety, love, and Belonging.

When I was a boy, and my mother's illness led her to reject my love, my safety and sense of worthiness were shaken to the point where I developed a lifelong relationship with depression. By inquiring into *her* experience, by the act and art of remembering who she truly was, I redeemed both my mother and myself. No longer unredeemable and unworthy of love, I became the redeemer.

This set off a cavalcade of acts of forgiveness. I forgave, for example, myself for my failings—as a father, a life partner, as a man but also as a leader. I forgave the sins of both commission and omission on the parts of both of my parents. I forgave the failures of my ancestors, especially their failure to live up to the values implicit in doing for the least of these.

In that forgiveness, I found myself easing my grip on urgency, productivity, and other forms of perfectionism, knowing well that I was far from irredeemable but, in fact, beloved of the divine. By letting go the perfectionism, I could see more clearly that, beyond even punishing myself for perceived failings, such structures supported supremacy, dominance of one group over another, head over heart.

Letting it go, I could see it more clearly. I could know with the felt sense of inclusivity that life is not to be colonized nor is happiness to be acquired.

Organizations centered on redemption and Belonging live that experience with daily acts of reparation. I spoke recently with a friend, the brilliant Annahid Dashtgard, author of *Breaking the Ocean: A Memoir of Race, Rebellion, and Reconciliation*, about the small daily acts possible when one lets go of perfection and other systems of Othering. "Micro-reparations," she called them, to our mutual delight. Simple daily acts of kindness and care, of seeing the world through the other's story, and relating empathically to our mutual longing to belong.

Micro-reparations, simple acts of using our empathic imagination to see and feel and be with the other, not to falsely equate the experience, say, of my suffering with that of those who might have endured systemic oppression but simply an act of heart-to-heart connection. From that heart connection, one sees the constancy of the need for a justice that repairs and restores, thus reuniting that which has been severed and separated.

Many years ago, after I had taken refuge in the Buddha, the dharma, and the sangha of my faith, I took my bodhisattva vows. In my faith, a bodhisattva is one who puts off release from suffering until all beings are free from suffering. It is a powerful pledge to do the work that may not be neglected even though the work may not be finished.

Being honest with myself, I tumbled my way into the dharma mostly to alleviate my own suffering. But the truth of the fundamental teachings left me thunderstruck: the path to the alleviation of that pain, that dukkha, is another through line; this time, however, it runs through the alleviation of suffering of others.

It turns out that this is also the through line to redemption and on to systemic Belonging. It may go by many names, including "leadership for the disinherited," "building beloved community," and, perhaps primarily, "using our power and privilege on behalf of the least of us," but it is all really about the alleviation of suffering. Such alleviation comes by way of reconciling with what has happened, a core principle in the redemptive power of repair.

When organizations hold a value of redemption, when they are committed to a policy in which failure and missteps are accompanied by curiosity, self-inquiry, and acceptance, then what arises is persistent, resilient Belonging.

THE BUSINESS OF BUSINESS IS BELONGING

When I was a kid, I read dozens of books on business; I was convinced that business was the path to riches, and riches would bring the safety I craved. This nerd would check out of the Brooklyn Public Library books on General Motors and ITT. I'll never forget the oft-quoted line about companies such as GM in the 1950s that the "business of America is business."

As an elder now, I see that it doesn't have to be that way. That view is, in fact, stultifying, nullifying, and annihilating— especially for the disinherited but also for all those who do not belong. What if the purpose of a business was to see people? What if our job as leaders was to pierce the cloak of invisibility, for example, that prevents white people from seeing nonwhite people, from straight people seeing gay people, from binary people seeing nonbinary? What if the responsibility of those in power was to see, feel, be with the disinherited and dispossessed? What if the true measure of a leader wasn't the toys they amassed, or the resources they extracted, but the lives they impacted positively? What if their legacy—something men in leadership often fixate on and worry about—were a legacy of inclusion? What if the purpose of our businesses, our enterprises—indeed *all* our endeavors—was to leave the world better than we found it and to leave the people with whom we lived and worked feeling loved, safe, and that they belong?

What if the business of a business was Belonging? What if a leader's job was to bring about jubilee?

What if the purpose of not just leadership but of all our human efforts was, in the end, to ensure that all belong—including and especially the dispossessed, the disinherited, and the wretched of the earth? What if *this* were the point of it all?

You don't have to finish the work, but you can't neglect it. We who strive to lead cannot heal all that ails the world, but we can heal more than we pretend. We are not as helpless as we've convinced ourselves. When companies embody the notion that otherness is not a threat but an opportunity, when the sacred promise of work is manifested in the ability of broken-open-hearted warriors doing the work of their lives, then all those with whom we spend our days will be somewhere they feel free. Being fierce with the reality that lies behind this truth is a cornerstone of not only better leadership but true adulthood. Even wise elderhood. Tactical, transactional management has a place in our societies and our organizations. We use these skills to build roadways and bridges, to ensure that we have clean drinking water and the vaccines necessary to protect from pandemics. But management that lacks a relationship to the deeper purpose of leadership ultimately fails to effect the changes in society necessary to give each of us the sense that we are loved, that we are safe, and that we belong.

HAVE I BEEN KIND? HAVE I SEEN NO STRANGERS?

Years ago, my friend and teacher Parker Palmer and I had a bellyful of laughs and good words for an episode of my podcast. In it, we swapped stories of folks asking repeatedly about the meaning of life. We said that perhaps the true measure of one's life was how one answered this question: Have I been kind?

Let's go further. Let's add to that by asking, Have I been kind not only to those with whom it's easy to be kind to? For example, those who look, think, believe, love, and practice the art of growing up as I do. But have I been kind to those with whom I disagree? Have I been kind to those who don't fit my narrative of "normal"? As Jesus taught, have I cared for the sick, the elderly, the downtrodden? But more, have I been kind to those imprisoned, disinherited, or otherwise Othered?

The writer Valerie Kaur has written of her Sikh faith as having at its basis a form of love where they are taught to "see no stranger." Imagine a world in which leadership was defined by seeing no strangers, by welcoming all, by using power to bend the arc of all endeavors toward justice, toward liberty, and toward Belonging for all.

In that space of fraught possibility, in this time of strife and reconsideration, in this time filled with the potential of jubilee, consider a few other variations on my complicity question: How might I be complicit in creating the world that I know is possible and that I'd like to see come into being? How can I put my shoulder to the wheel of systemic Belonging? How might I make this year, and the years to come, a jubilee?

And after my inner journey to my own Belonging is far enough along, how might I turn my attention to the outer journey, so that my actions as a leader, as one who holds power, reflect my feelings with grace and integrity, allowing me to become an active co-conspirator in the fostering of systemic Belonging?

Over the years, in countless interviews, I asked such questions again and again. One struck a nerve, and it has reverberated back at me hundreds of times over.

For years I've asked folks to consider how they have been complicit in creating the conditions they say they don't want. And the question was repeated, often directly and occasionally in distorted ways, hundreds of times. When I saw the reaction to that question, I knew I was speaking a redeeming, reconciling, and reparative truth. I knew that I was doing what I set out to do when I made a promise to my daughter, Emma, and her brothers, Sam and Michael; I knew I was using my God-given gift to string a few words together and cause hearts to ripple and flutter and minds to open. I knew I was beginning to make good on the promise I made to a daughter who, fearing COVID, pepper spray, and riot gear–equipped police, acted on the belief that all people belong, all people, without exception.

My fierce daughter was willing to put her body on the line, to give up an expectation of safety. What was I willing to give up? My status? My inclusion in a beloved class of elders who had somehow given the impression of having transcended the bounds of my own racism and proclivity for Othering.

That better humans make better leaders is both radically obvious and undeniably true; still, as an insight it falls short of fostering the changes in the world that need to occur. It is true *and* insufficient. Given the backs against the walls, the many knees and feet on necks, and the growing number of the disinherited and dispossessed, it's not enough to be a better human. It is not enough to be an ally. Leadership in business and society demands that we actively and systemically work on behalf of those who have been Othered.

There are plagues being visited upon our home and infecting our family. These contagions share a root belief in the need to systemically Other those who are different from the dominant cohort. The plague of nationalism in service to racism and a perversion of religious beliefs where religion divides instead of fulfilling the obligations of the bond with the divine has lit the world on fire.

While it is true that we have always Othered the other, it is also true that the contagion is growing once more. Love, safety, and Belonging for all are the only things that will quench the flames, contain the contagions.

In writing of Sikhism's core belief to see no stranger, Kaur defines the quest as a bid for radical love. This feels as much a manifestation of the *religare* of religion as Dr. King's world house and beloved community. Kaur's reflection recalls Jesus's pleading for the "least of these" and the Buddha's invocations that begin with "may all beings" as in "may all beings belong."

For all means all, even those locked away, disregarded, disinherited, and dismembered from the hand that is society.

This isn't "woke." This isn't a fad; it is life and death. Our silence equals death, and our Belonging brings life.

The work of Belonging can be deeply satisfying, especially when the fear is replaced by a loving, joyful, and beloved curiosity about the Other. It is only by the reunification with those whose backs have been against the wall that we can resurrect that which is whole and good about us as a species. The response to the lack of compassion and love isn't fear and authoritarianism, it's love. This is the leader's response to the longing for Belonging.

It is only through this reunion that we may bring forth the conditions we want to see in the world: a world house, a radical love, a beloved community, and, finally, persistent, consistent, everlasting, and, indeed, radically systemic Belonging.

CHAPTER 8

Reunion

41.
when angels speak of love
they tell us
all is union and reunion
dying reborn again
there is no separation
no end to paradise
we are always present
the ecstatic moving us
along each current
each wilderness of spirit
a dedicated path

—BELL HOOKS

Sometimes the breeze blows and, when it does, it gently rocks paper cranes placed on the black granite of a 9/11 Memorial, honoring the memories of loved ones lost to the wages of separation. Sometimes the breeze blows and carries with it the words of a poet, a descendant of those Indigenous to this land, born under the same sky. Quoting a poet, the breeze might say, "Remember the sky you were born under . . . Remember the sun's birth at dawn."

Such memories, coming on the winds, are gifts. They bring understanding. They bring an appreciation that turns ghosts into ancestors. And sometimes when the breeze arrives, it carries whispers from the other side. In those whispers, if we listen closely, we can hear our ancestors speak as angels might: "These are the stars under which you were born, this is from whence you've come, and to whom you belong. *This* is who you are."

By such whispers, then, they might, like elders, guide us to what it is we are to do with that which has been given us. Ghosts becoming ancestors and ancestors becoming elders.

Such angels, such long-missing elders who dwell not far and just on the other side, guide our hearts and our feet, showing us the ways to our Belonging.

For when poets speak of angels, they tell us not only about ourselves but of those who came before—their lives, their heartbreak, and, mostly, their longing to belong. When elder angels speak of love, they speak of reconciliation, reparation, redemption, and reunion.

For whispered poetry is one way to overcome the wages of separation. But to hear such songs, we must venture out and back in time. We must go to the places of our ancestors so that we may listen to that which they heard, see what they saw, and feel the kiss on the cheek of the breezes of home.

DUBLIN

I'd come to Dublin from Wales. I'd been visiting the United Kingdom—London first, and then the small town of Cardigan, Wales. It was my first overseas trip since just before the start of the pandemic.

As I told the taxi driver who'd picked me up at the airport for the trip to my hotel, I'd returned to Dublin, intent on visiting the Old Graveyard at Moycarkey. I fingered the smooth velvet of the tiny package containing a rosary blessed by Pope Francis, too precious to be left to my checked luggage.

My grandmother, I explained, to the nodding driver. She gave birth in America, I explained further. "Indeed," he said, nodding. "There's more than a few like her and even more like you who come back."

Back? I pondered silently. Am I back? Yes, I'd been to Ireland before—to Dublin, even—but is this the *return* that my driver speaks of?

"Yeah, there's more than a few," the driver repeated as he stared straight ahead, letting his words hang a bit. After a pause he added, "And more than a few who left someone there as much as they left someone here."

Another brief silence. The cool air of Ireland was a relief from the heat I'd left in London. He spoke again. "So, it's County Tipperary, is it?" he asked, continuing without letting me reply. "There's more than a few who made it there from other places back then, back all the way to the famine."

I nodded, thinking of the guess my genealogist and guide, Brian, had made about my ancestors having migrated in the 1800s. To find work. To find shelter. To find food.

"I wouldn't be surprised," Brian had offered when we'd communicated before my trip, "if the Heffernans"—my father's mother's family—"weren't originally from in and around Thurles," the largest town in the area. The town central to Moycarkey, Ballymoreen, Parkstown, and Galbooly. They likely moved from the west, east to Tipperary. "Ah, yes . . . they may have even walked the famine roads."

The famine roads. Crisscrossing the landscape, zigzagging up and down hills, are incomplete "roads"—visible reminders of the policies of a distant overseer government whose offer to the starving Irish peasantry was the "work" of building such roads to nowhere in exchange for bread, milk, or a few potatoes. A nineteenth-century equivalent of the twentieth-century American policy of "workfare." In lieu of support from the state, instead of support from the community, those with their backs to the wall were forced to earn their bread. Because, of course, the poor, the disinherited, and the starving couldn't simply have been fed, sheltered, and clothed. No, under the nineteenth-century Poor Law, they had to work to pay the wages of separation that cost them their lives, cost them their children. Roads to nowhere and workhouses for those with knees on their necks and backs against the wall.

"So, it's back to County Tipperary, is it?" my driver repeated, using the mirror to catch my eyes and break my reverie.

WRITERS AT THE BAR

A few hours after landing at the airport, I'd met Joy-Tendai at the Bar of Ireland, the professional association of barristers, based at the Law Library. In the time since we'd met during my last visit to Dublin, in the time in which she'd noted that my story was her story, Joy-Tendai had become a barrister.

She and some friends—a few aspiring writers—had asked if I'd do a reading from *Reboot*. After that reading, I shared a few pages from a draft of this book. I was nervous. I feared the consequences of my speaking of things which many prefer left unspoken—of knees on necks, backs against walls, and the disinheriting of our ancestors. I feared being told that I shouldn't mention such things, despite being in a city that preserved the bullet holes in public spaces, left by the conquering forces of an army sent to crush a people who wanted to belong to a free republic.

Nothing can be changed unless it is faced, I reminded them, paraphrasing James Baldwin. "Are we willing to face ourselves, our history, and the myths and fables of our ancestors?" I asked. "If not, how will anything change?"

I noted that I'd written in a different voice than I'd written with before. "It's angry," I told them. "And I want you to be angry as well." Injustice walks the famine roads, I reminded them, and death stalks the walls of separation.

I shared what I've come to know about the ways of immigrants—their emigrant ancestors as well as my immigrant kin—dissolved into a projected ideal of that myth of exceptionalism, and the mythic melting pot of sameness. Their relatives and mine, in the movements away from the famine roads and toward the streets paved with possibility, were absorbed, dissolved, and made whiter than white by the myths of exceptionalism, sameness, and equal opportunity for all.

"Life, liberty, and the pursuit of happiness," I said, "the myth that drew my ancestors and yours was that the pursuit of happiness was available to all." The fable rooted in the phrase "for all" when the reality was and still is "for some."

The resulting movement toward whiteness—for my ancestors from the irredeemable southern Italy and the less-than-human Éire—to America, the land that despised them even as it exploited their labor to build their cities, monuments to these myths.

Over pints, I mused: For all, for all, for all . . . it never was for all, but if folks like me do our work, it might yet be.

MOYCARKEY

I went to Moycarkey to listen to the dead.

Having written of the things about which I hadn't wanted to know, having imagined what it might have been like for my father—the boy with two names—to have felt unclaimed by his birth mother, Mary Heffernan, I remained unsettled. While reuniting with the facts of my father's ancestry—and, consequently, the facts of my own, filled the negative space of my own father hunger, my own felt sense of love, safety, and Belonging remained less than fulfilled. The negative space of an absent elder was still a hole in my chest.

So I went to the final resting place of Mary Heffernan, my father's mother, my grandmother. I went to the Old Graveyard, hard by the white-and-gray St. Peter's Church in Moycarkey, County Tipperary. I went to commune with my dead ancestors, to feel their presence, to remember the sky under which they'd lived. I went and felt the same breeze that kissed their cheeks as they were baptized, married, and laid to rest. I went to stand in the light as it can slant only in that place, dappling like shook gold the leaves of the trees. I went to stir memories, dormant but still present in my body. I went to present their descendant, to say, "It's me, I live, and I remember you. You are here and I am here."

Joy-Tendai had connected me with the genealogist Brian who, working with the little information I had, found the burial records of my grandmother. What's more, he found some of my grandmother's ancestors—that is, *my* ancestors—as well.

I remember scanning the emailed document the genealogist sent, my breath catching, as her name jumped out at me. "Here. Here she is."

Months later, I sat next to Joy-Tendai, frozen. In the car park beside the churchyard, after the long drive from Dublin, I was unable to step out of the car. I was afraid—of what, I wasn't sure. After decades of denying my father's true birth, after a lifetime of angry dismissals of the woman who'd given him up, I was afraid, perhaps, of what I might find in the gravel-covered churchyard. I was afraid of what I would feel.

"It feels like our ancestors brought us together," Joy-Tendai said, breaking the silence. It felt as if our ancestors were conspiring to bring us to that churchyard, under its bright sky and cool breezes. I nodded.

The thought of our ancestors, angels in death however they were in life, guiding us here and to this place comforted me.

Resolved, I stepped from the car and walked through the stiff, noisily turning wrought-iron gate onto the gravel-covered soil, the resting places of my ancestors. Slowly, reverently, timidly, we walked among the graves, in and around stones of various sizes, in varying degrees of weathered decay.

I walked over the bones of my kin.

I couldn't find my family. I couldn't find a single name from the family trees painstakingly constructed by others before me. I was sad. But if I'm honest, I was also relieved.

I considered how I would integrate this experience, just as it was. Standing in the churchyard, the drama of the moment falling flat. "I couldn't find anyone," I would tell my partner, Ali; my kids; my brothers and my sisters. But I would describe the churchyard, the trip, and my futile attempt to find Dad's biological mother. It would be a footnote in my journey to Belonging.

It would be a family reunion that simply hadn't happened.

"Here they are!" shouted Joy-Tendai. Shocked, I sprinted to where she was pointing. "Here they are." I was overwhelmed with . . . disappointment, disappointment rooted in the apprehension I'd felt about what might happen were I to find the grave. She saw it in my eyes.

"You looked like you were about to give up," she said.

I stood before a grave marker that was, perhaps, five feet high. "Here she is," I repeated to myself. "Here she is."

"There's more than a few that come back." I recalled my taxi driver's words. I was now part of a new clan; I'd come back.

A Celtic cross topped the stone, and carved into the center of the cross was a crowned heart—the sacred heart of Jesus. Just below, lacking any weathering whatsoever, were seven names, five of whom were Heffernans. The last name on the list, the name closest to the pedestal and just inches above the carved "R.I.P.," was my father's mother, my grandmother, the woman who—however briefly she held him—claimed him by naming him William Michael Heffernan.

Above her were the names of her mother, Ellen; her father, Patrick. She shared the plot with her aunt, uncle, sister, and brother-in-law. For some, below their names and the dates of their passing, were the dates and places of their births—Parkstown and Ballymoreen. Ballymoreen, the tiny town not far from Moycarkey, where a 1911 census placed my then four-year-old grandmother in a household headed by her father and joined by her mother, her brother, her sister, and her maternal grandmother—my great-grandmother. The building, a thatched-roof two-room cottage, lacking water and glazing in the one window, sheltered five people.

It comforted me to know she was not alone.

Ballymoreen, Ballymoreen, Ballymoreen: the name reverberates in my body. The soil, the land, the slant of the light of Ballymoreen . . . I need to remember it all, for it flows through me; and through me it flows to my children and, eventually, to their children.

I took a knee and ran a hand through the gravel, feeling the need to hold the earth of my kin.

We looked around and noticed more Heffernans. Thomas, Patrick's brother, and his family, buried just to the right, his marker less ornate but no less resilient to the weather. Thomas, place of birth, the parish of Galbooly. Slowly, slowly—with my eyes adjusting to the shifting light of that now cloud-filled sky, I looked around and took in the land, listening for my angels.

We agreed to go check into our hotel, The Horse and Jockey Inn, near Parkstown. We agreed to come back the next day.

CLAIMING MY GRANDMOTHER

Before sleeping, I called my partner, Ali, from my room at the inn and shared with her the day. "I needed to claim her," I told her. "I needed her to know that this descendant, among many, would travel to visit her grave."

Ali replied, "You need to let her know you didn't forget her."

I'd once pushed away the knowledge of her. I'd once left unclaimed all these laborers, farmers, carpenters, and stable hands. In doing so, I had denied my having descended from the famine roads. In doing so, I had denied some of the people to whom I belonged.

In coming back, in reuniting with these dead generations, I was completing a circle, like the cross that encircles the sacred heart.

The second morning in Tipperary was overcast and slightly chilly. We left the hotel and stopped in Thurles. I wanted to bring flowers to my grandmother's grave.

I'd slept fitfully the previous night. I dreamed that my sister Nicki and I were picking through trinkets and souvenirs from the hotel's gift shop. Paying for the items, I told the cashier the reason for our visit, expecting the sort of welcome the taxi driver had given me. Instead, the cashier blushed. Other shoppers, overhearing the story of my grandmother who'd given birth out of wedlock, were hushed into a collective shame. Nicki leaned into me, protecting me but cautioning me as well, "We don't speak of such things." I woke, felt ashamed, and joined Joy-Tendai for breakfast.

We arrived early to the florist in Thurles. Annie's Blooms would not open for another few minutes. So we walked the main street. I took in the river, the arts center, an imposing church, and the affiliated school.

We returned to the shop just as Annie unlocked the door. Looking around, I felt a bit fazed and lost. I explained to Annie why I'd come. Like the taxi driver, she nodded in recognition. But as much as she shared that my story, my grandmother's story, was a familiar story—there was a slight blush that seemed to carry the same shame about which I had dreamed.

"We don't speak of such things."

There is so much of which families don't speak.

I pointed to white roses and asked what she thought of my leaving a bouquet with my grandmother. Kindly, she noted that such flowers would wilt in the heat that was to come. She steered me to a set of potted fake flowers. One pot, with fake white roses, was black and heavy and sported a faux-brass plaque with the words *In Loving Memory* engraved in the plastic.

Its heft was satisfying. "It won't blow away," I told myself. "It'll stay put even when the storms come."

But fake flowers felt wrong. "Real flowers will just wilt in the heat," Annie repeated. Then added a reassuring, "The permanent flowers are what folks do." She had heard my story with kind eyes that helped memorialize the dead of Tipperary, the North Riding, the country surrounding Thurles. Real roses in one hand, fake in another, I did what I often do in such circumstances; I chose both.

We drove back to the churchyard, and this time I was alone to wander among the bones of my ancestors, my kin. I placed the bouquet of white roses beside the tall headstone and the black plastic pot at its base.

I prayed and spoke with her, my grandmother. I fed the silver rosary with blue sapphires through the empty spaces at the top of the stone, leaving the tiny silver crucified Christ resting against the carved crown and sacred heart.

I weeded the grave site, pulling thistles by their roots from the gravel and soil. I pocketed a discarded cigarette packet, wondering who had smoked while they'd visited, wondering if they were a cousin lost to the shame of out-of-wedlock births, to family secrets that denied the reunions that are our birthright and responsibility.

"We don't speak of such things."

I thought of the Buddha asking the earth to bear witness to his enlightenment as I touched the earth, my own earth-touching mudra, the gravel and soil of Moycarkey bearing witness to my reunion.

Twirling thistles through my fingers, I sat on my haunches and told my grandmother of her son and of his children and of their children. I told her of her fierce-as-fuck great-granddaughter who had spent her high school years exploring abolitionists, and who'd decided, after college, to put her shoulder to the wheel of social justice by teaching.

I spoke of my sons, strong and good men each, with brave and big hearts and curious minds. I spoke of the irony of one son's unwitting reunion with Ireland through his semester of study at Trinity College. I told her about our wanderings through Dublin and how it evoked memories of my father, her son, his grandfather.

I spoke even further of my father. I shared his troubles with alcohol, for example—something about which I suspect she was familiar, as more than a few of our ancestors had been jailed for public drunkenness. But I also told her of my father's love of jigsaw puzzles, Westerns, and history. And I told of his service in World War II when, after the combat had ended, he'd been part of a team at the army's *Stars and Stripes* newspaper, while the war crimes trials at Nuremberg began. I shared, too, his dedication to veterans, his sometimes-weekly visits to the local Veterans Administration hospital, where he would bring his used puzzles and listen to other men's stories of war.

I spoke of his passing. I spoke of my anger. I spoke of his lost and sometimes empty and bloodshot blue eyes. ("Did he inherit those from you, Grandma?") I spoke of his shame and wordless suffering at my mother's tirades. And I spoke of his steadfastness despite his obvious heartache; how he never left us—the whole clan of his seven kids and his hurting wife—despite what I can only imagine was his longing to belong somewhere, anywhere other than there. Somewhere and to someone.

I sat before the headstone and let her know what she had left behind. I gave her permission, what permission it was mine to give, to rest knowing her son made it and that his children and grandchildren and great-grandchildren were all wondrous humans about whom she could be proud.

Looking up and around at more gravestones, something shifted. As a boy I had steadfastly denied my Irish heritage. Even as my father struggled with his own depression, even as he lost himself in beer and puzzles, I rejected what was true.

Slowly, then, as I scanned the headstones, I began to claim kinship with not only the Heffernans born in Ballymoreen and Galbooly and buried in Moycarkey but all those who traveled the famine roads. I looked up in remembrance and kinship with those who refused to pay the Church of Ireland in the Tithe War, the attempt to nonviolently overthrow the overlords from across the Irish Sea.

I claimed them just as I had been proud to claim kinship with those who rubbed fish on pieces of bread while Christ the Redeemer seemed to have abandoned them at Eboli, going no farther on Italy's famine road. I claimed Mary Heffernan's grandfather, John, who had to rely on the kindness of the Catholic Church in Ireland to feed and house his children. I claimed his father, Patrick, who had his own struggles with the law. I claimed them all.

I claimed as kin, for example, if not as an ancestor, one Patrick Heffernan, convicted of a no-doubt minor crime born out of poverty created by their overlords and transported to Australia in 1810. He may or may not have been an ancestor; he died in that foreign land; he traversed the famine roads; he—like more than a few—endured the Irish middle passage.

I claimed the neighbor whose headstone marked his birth and his death but noted that his body reposes in faraway North Dakota. "Here lies Thomas," read another stone, "his brother Patrick remembered here but interred in London."

Here but not here—the scars of diaspora so common to the disinherited everywhere. The words of my taxi driver drifted back: "And more than a few who left someone there as much as they left someone here."

I knelt and prayed, not the Catholic rituals of my childhood, not the Our Fathers and Hail Marys imposed upon me as a boy in contrition for imagined sins, but the poems of my adulthood. Words that were no less sacred and holy. I prayed the poem "Vespers" by John O'Donohue, the former Irish priest, the teacher who taught me of the *anam cara*—the soul friend—and the power of Celtic love and Gaelic words amid broken-open-hearted lamentations for the dead generations.

In so doing, I sought to find communion, union, and reunion with these elder kin.

Kneeling in the gravel, I thought of my other grandmother Nicoletta Guido, saying her novena to Mary, the mother of Jesus. And I thought of my father's adopted mother, also Mary. As I sat before the grave of this grandmother, Mary, I thought of the adoration of the Virgin Mary. She who is the access point to the Christ, the true Christ, the redeemer.

This Mary, whose bones were before me, became the access point to my ancestors and kin and the dead generations stretching back as far as time might remember.

It wasn't just for her that I prayed. As I gripped the soil, read of the peace of vespers, stared at the sapphire and silver rosary, hanging about the sacred heart, I prayed for myself. As I prayed for the peace that comes at the end of the day, the dead generations turned from ghosts to ancestors and to elders and angels, no longer haunting me for the simple reason that I remembered them. With flowers, fake and real.

We left Moycarkey and visited Galbooly. There, near the entrance to the ghostly and abandoned townlet was a single hydrant, whose once bright red paint was now peeling. It took little to imagine my grandmother as a girl being told to be good and fetch a pail down at the hydrant, the only source of water a deep well beneath the soil of the land of my ancestors and kin.

I stood in the lane that wound its way through a half dozen shells of homes, long abandoned, and heard the words of James Joyce: "Once upon a time and a very good time it was there was a moocow coming down along the road and this moocow that was coming down along the road met a nicens little boy named baby tuckoo."

Amid the tumbled bones of the homes of my kin, I imagined myself a "nicens little boy" waiting for the "moocow" so we might have a bit of milk.

Amid the overgrown lane and tumbled bones, I heard the voices of the past. The lives of my ancestors, my elders speaking as if on the wind. I heard their voices and I heard the voices that were spoken to them.

"Jerry, sweetie," says Grandma Guido, "take my scissors and cut me a rose for our breakfast table . . . and grab a fig while you're out. But careful as you reach."

"Jerry, see that lady?" says Grandpa Guido. "See that statue? See that torch? That lady, standing in the harbor . . . she'll always welcome you. So always put your hand over your heart when you see her."

"Come on, Jerry," says Marcus on a hot summer morning as he leans into the window of our ground-floor apartment. "Come on! I got a new Spaldeen."

"Mary, be a nicens little girl and fetch us some water from the hydrant."

On this summer morning, in the lanes of Galbooly, I not only claimed the dead generations of my Irish kin but, in doing so, could reach back in time and claim my father, his mother, and my brother Marcus, lost to the wages of separation.

It was as if I were able to remember the soil and the sky under which the dead generations were buried. In remembering, I redeemed the sacred hearts of my kinfolk, and my restless lack of Belonging began to quiet. I was home.

"We are born and have our being in a place of memory," wrote bell hooks in *Belonging*. "We chart our lives by everything we remember from the mundane moment to the majestic." Memories, offered the poet, deliver us a world free from death, one in which we are sustained by rituals of regard and recollection.

I went to Moycarkey to commune with the dead, to remember them and no longer deny them. I went to Moycarkey to know what I didn't want to know, to feel what I didn't want to feel so that I could write what I needed to write so that I might live up to my daughter's exhortation of being a co-conspirator of Belonging.

I went to Moycarkey to evoke the place that lives in my

body as a distant memory. I went to Moycarkey to remember not only my ancestors but the clay and gravel that hold their bones. I went to Moycarkey to regard my ancestors and ended up recollecting their lives. I went home.

HIRAETH

One day, a few years back, a Welsh friend, Wil, taught me a word that gave voice to a feeling I was struggling to express. "Hiraeth," he said casually, as I described the combination of bittersweet longing for a place that may or may never have been visited. That longing and the heartache of wanting to belong to a soil, a slant of light, the way a breeze shakes and dapples leaves like gold in sunlight.

"Hiraeth," he repeated, conjuring for me the broken hearts of Celtic cousins gripped by a dominator, settler mindset and, for far too many, forced into mines so their shortened lives and racked bodies might carry blackened lungs into the fresh air coming in off the Irish Sea.

Hiraeth is a longing for the Belonging of the soil of our ancestors, and kin, and for the sacred heart of a grandmother who could have made my own sad father's heart a little lighter with the knowledge of his own Belonging. "If only my father could have come," I said to the shadows like wind and the sky and the ivy-covered stones and weathered markers. If only he could have come and planted his knee as I have done and told his mother that he was well, despite having been left, despite having been unnamed and unclaimed by his father. He was well and had done his best. And, with my mother, he raised seven children into adulthood and bounced a few grandkids on his knees.

Listening to my Celtic heart, I realize that Hiraeth is more than a longing for the soil and gravel of the graves at Moycarkey. It is the wish to let the soil slip through my fingers and mix with the long-dried fig juice making my fingers sticky when, as a boy, I picked the fruit of my ancestors and their ancestors and their ancestors before them. The sapling on Beverly Road brought from miles away in the hills of Puglia, surrounding Palo del Colle.

Hireath is the sound of pink Spaldeens bounce, bounce, bouncing on East Twenty-Sixth in Brooklyn. It's the swipe of a skully cap gliding across a board carved into the asphalt under the shade of a chestnut tree, the crack of which is just big enough to shelter a lost little boy, hiding from the violence of his home.

Hireath is the feeling that overwhelmed me as I walked the estuaries in Cardigan, Wales, with my son, Sam—a grown man; the waving reedy cattails watered by the Irish Sea. A few days earlier, at a festival on a farm, one hundred or so people gathered in a weathered stone barn and listened as I read from this still-in-progress work. Hireath is the look on my son's face as he sat upright in the back of the barn. Our eyes meeting after I read of knees on necks and the need for leaders to work toward Belonging for all.

"I'm proud of you," he whispered as he embraced me. Hireath is the longing for the pride of a son who has every reason to question the wisdom and integrity of his father but chooses to bond with the blood and the soil upon which his father stands. In that space, in that embrace between ancestor and descendant, is reunion.

Returning to Ireland, heeding the call of reunion, I remembered the pain of the famine roads and reconnected to the degradation of the land abandoned by Christ, the land below Eboli, land of my kin, the *meridionali* whose whiteness, and therefore welcome, was questioned by the powers that be in the land of their dreams. I allowed their pain to sweep me away and called each place home.

I belong there, hard by the gray-and-white church in Moycarkey, and on the ancient lane hard by the faded red hydrant at Galbooly, among the ruins of thatched cottages. But I also belong to the hills outside Bari, in the Place of the Column: Palo del Colle. And I belong to the tan brick house on Beverly Road, with the fig tree and roses in the back. And I belong to East Twenty-Sixth Street, in Brooklyn, especially when the hot asphalt is drenched and cooled by the waters of an open fire hydrant.

LIBERATING THE DEAD GENERATIONS

As I've written, it is both true and insufficient to say that better humans make better leaders. It is true because the core of any good leadership is understanding, through radically inquiring within, the ways and means of our subroutines, our core beliefs and how they create love, safety, and—ideally—Belonging for those whom we are privileged to lead.

But it is also insufficient if it fails to declare the unequivocable intention of leadership: better humans who lead well must understand the heartbreaking wages of separation. More, though, they must also seek to unite and reunite those dismembered by extractive forces that exploit division and capitalize on Othering. For, as bell hooks wrote, in the end "all is union and reunion." In that place of reunion, there is no separation, no end of paradise. And in that paradise, the remembered ghosts become ancestors and ancestor-angels speak only of love.

"The arduous task of being a human," wrote the Irish poet John O'Donohue, "is to balance longing and belonging so that they work with and against each other to ensure that all the potential and gifts that sleep in the clay of the heart may be awakened and realized in this one life." To be a better human and better leaders means taking up that mantle and that task. Doing so is not a burden but an honor.

Leading for the disinherited means balancing longing and Belonging for ourselves, yes. But, most importantly, it also means doing the work of reunion precisely for those for whom we are called to lead. We must use our own reunion and communion with elder angels to reunite the disinherited with their inheritance, to awaken that which sleeps in the soil of places like Galbooly.

The Italians in New Orleans were lynched partly because of the accusation of murdering a "white" sheriff but, too, they had committed the offense of doing business, living with, and in some cases marrying the children of the formerly enslaved. The movement of my kin from natural allies of the disinherited to rivals or enemies coincided with the movement toward acceptance in the dominant culture and the safety it brings.

Whiteness served to separate, which then served dominance, which in turn served the economic status quo. That movement toward whiteness by my kin—if not all my ancestors—built those walls of separateness. This is how my kin, if not my ancestors, were complicit in the Othering of others. This is how my kin benefited from that which I say I do not want to see in the world.

This is how we are all complicit in the conditions of the

world we say we do not want. Our silence about this furthers our complicity. We should be grateful for the sacrifices our ancestors made. We should acknowledge all who have paid, and continue to pay, these wages, the price of our ancestors' and our descendants' tickets to love, safety, and Belonging.

If I am going to claim kinship with these people and this land, with the shady lanes of Galbooly and the weathered headstones of Moycarkey, as well as the back lanes and surrounding villages of New Orleans and the fig and olive trees of Palo del Colle, then I must claim kinship with *all* my ancestors and *all they have done*. Seeing the ways they were Othered makes them martyrs to Belonging. But if I see *only* their Othering, then I end up maintaining the systems I say I don't want to exist in the world.

Being a better human means we must also claim the ways they Othered, the ways we all benefited from systemic non-Belonging as my ancestors—from Ireland as well as from Italy—moved toward the safety and tenuously held Belonging of whiteness.

By knowing my kin, by seeing them, by feeling the rough pricks of the thistles' thorns as I weeded the family grave site; by picking through the soil of Moycarkey, of Horse and Jockey, of Parkstown, of Galbooly and Ballymoreen; by walking the paths and seeing the remains of what had been thatched rooms where the dead generations had birthed, healed the sick, grown old, and where they keened the dead, sending them to St. Peter's in Moycarkey to be anointed and sent further on; the famine road leading away from degradation, disenfranchisement, disinherited from the land of their ancestors . . . by seeing all this, by tasting the waters of the deeply sunk well of Galbooly that watered and baptized and nourished and cleansed their famished, disinherited bodies, I turned these ghosts into ancestors so that I might be a descendant worthy of their love.

If I am going to live up to the challenge laid at my feet by my fierce daughter, and be a worthy ancestor to her, her brothers, and their descendants, then I must work toward understanding the ongoing story of my Belonging so that my story may be another's story of Belonging. For the story of each finger on that hand is another's story of Belonging.

A DEDICATION OF THE MERIT

In my Buddhist lineage we're taught to dedicate whatever merit our actions may have generated. I dedicate, therefore, whatever small bit of merit my labors have generated to the generations who lived, and continue to live, with the bitter consequences of disinheritance and Othering. I hope this small merit moves backs from the walls, and knees or feet from necks, and welcomes home the least of these. For whatever happened, whatever happens, to the least of us is my concern, my responsibility, my duty to address. In this way, and only in this way, can I live up and into my aspiration to be a better human.

For those who identify as I do—white, cisgender male, straight, especially those who resonated with my story, seeing my story as their story—I ask you to consider some simple questions: How have you been complicit in, and benefited from, systems of oppression that Othered others? More importantly, though, what is it that your ancestors, your elders, are saying that is your work to do?

Even the most exalted of us belong to, and with, the least of these. Their stories *are* our stories. We are not the same, but we are part of the same hand. When we forget that, when we sever ourselves from each other, death comes. When we re-member, angels will speak of love and elders will sing of our Belonging. And descendants will dream their way through shame and into the loving arms of Belonging.

We don't know each other because we don't hear each other. And because we've not been heard, generations of us fail to explore who we truly are, to whom we belong, and from whence we came. Those of us seeing the world from the vantage point of privilege and the safety of dominance are called upon by our elders, our ancestors, and the disinherited to question the myths of roots, the reality of our Belonging. The price of the ticket of privilege is to ignore the calls of our ancestors turned elders, the angels who guide us.

So therefore, we do not see the other, do not know their stories. At best, we gin up sympathy—the tsk-tsk that passes for care. By failing to know the truth of our journey, our trans-generational longing to belong, we fail to embrace the primordial empathy that defines us as humans. We fail to know that their stories are our stories. We then become unwitting participants in the great Othering. We fail to see the humans before our eyes, people with backs against the wall and knees on their necks.

This book began with a knee on the neck. It ends with a knee in the dirt and gravel and flowers—real and fake—at a grave. It ends with hope that the life that comes from overcoming the walls of separation, reuniting with that which was severed, will spread to all, living up to the true meaning of the American creed that all are created equal, and all deserve the inclusivity that is the felt sense of love, safety, and Belonging.

It also ends with a path forward. It ends with a way to manifest the exhortation of a young woman to her father. This path is simple but hard: acknowledge the truth of your own becoming, the path to your own Belonging, so that you might use your agency and power to respond to the longing to Belong of others.

Doing this requires that we see past the myths and fables that protect us, to the truth of our lives and the lives that came before us. In doing so, we may then hear the stories of the disinherited so that we may know that their story is our story.

By such union with that truth, this book ends with reunion: with ourselves, with our ancestors and kinfolk, with the land of our true homes, and, most of all, with each other.

There is hope in reunion, more so even than in union. Reunion implies a return. Reunion speaks of returning to a time when we—all of us—were together, when there was no separation, when two eight-year-old boys would love each other and lived in separate rooms of the world house, before the adults' need to divide and separate made them fear each other.

All things are union and reunion, and, in that space, there is no end to paradise. Such reunion is more than a process of reconciliation, more than a call for repair, more, even, than a wish for renewal. It is all that and more. In the paradise of reunion, a promise from our elder angels that, if we speak of and live into our birthright of love, then there will be no separation. And, absent separation, the wages of love will become life itself.

DEDICATION OF MERIT

And now as long as space endures,
as long as there are beings to be found,
may I likewise remain,
to drive away the sorrows of the world.
—Shantideva

Holding Stories of Belonging

I first understood the power of holding others' stories more than a decade ago when I was on fast in a Utah desert. Sitting still, with only the land and the boulders as my wise elder witnesses, I realized my true calling: the work that I am not allowed to neglect is to listen and hold the stories of others. I left that desert with a new name: Holder of Stories of the Heart.

Now, after nearly three years of exploring a leader's responsibility for creating systemic Belonging, I've seen that these stories of the heart are mostly stories of the longing to Belong.

In the introduction, I asked that you treat the journey of reading this book as if you were attending a workshop. I wrote:

Workshops work because they create emotional experiences, necessary components for any transformation. Cognitive awareness of the need to confront systemic Othering, with carefully constructed arguments, is vital. But it is only a first step. If it is not followed by a felt sense of the need for change—in this case, the tangible, emotional, financial costs of disunion—then change becomes a labor of forced intellect. It becomes performative.

The way to feel that need to change, then, is for you to be your own version of Holder, to listen to the longing of those all around you and, after doing so, consider your own longings.

As with any good workshop, this exercise should provoke you. It might make you uncomfortable, for example. Or it might make you sad; looking at what's been kept secret is difficult and painful. There's safety in not talking about the dismembered parts of ourselves or our families. Searching for the branches missing from our family trees might provoke profound grief, especially when those missing are lost because of the wages of separation such as enforced diaspora and negation.

I have a small sense of that pain because my tree remains incomplete. For example, I have yet to overcome my anger at my father's biological father for his unwillingness to claim my father, and so he remains a missing branch. I hope someday to be brave enough to learn his story and the stories of his father before him. I might then better understand a father who refuses to claim his child.

If practices such as this are done with love and kindness, it will also provoke a deep dialogue with yourself and, eventually, with others. And that is the point of reunion. My hope is to provoke the dialogue that will lead to persistent, systemic Belonging.

We will never overcome the walls of separation until we hear one another's stories of Belonging.

Working with three dear friends, I tried to re-create that experience by inviting each of them to share their stories of Belonging. Think of us all sitting in a large circle, sharing our stories. As you read each story, consider each person a wildflower. Each story, each person, is unique in the way they've responded to the light and water they've received and the soil in which they were planted.

The first essay is by Virginia Baumann. A colleague of mine at the company I co-founded, Reboot. Virginia works with leaders to bring more of themselves to every situation that leadership demands. A trained software engineer, she's been building companies ever since she graduated from college. She believes her identity plays no small part in her coaching and is called on to support organizations which, in turn, support underrepresented people; in this work she hopes to instill a lasting sense of Belonging for all.

The second essay is by Chrystal Bell, another Reboot coach. Prior to training as a coach, Chrystal spent twenty years in forensics as a crime scene examiner for the Oregon State Police. Despite having seen the worst of what humans can do to one another, she holds an enduring belief in the possibility of healing, belonging, and connection, even in the most difficult places.

The third essay is by my dear friend Joy-Tendai Kangere. A barrister specializing in Employment and Labor law at the Bar of Ireland, Joy-Tendai is a fierce advocate for justice, equity, diversity, and inclusion (JEDI), and a founder of Roots in Africa-Ireland. Born in Zimbabwe, and now calling Ireland home, she is inspired by the African principle of ubuntu ("I am because we are") to use her voice to elevate everyone with whom she connects.

Unique and precious, their stories are theirs alone. And yet, like fingers on a hand, their stories are also part of a collective story. Their stories are our stories.

SPEAKING THE UNSPOKEN AND NAMING
THE UNNAMED: VIRGINIA'S STORY

I was born in 1983. It took me a long time to come out to my family. I had to move across the United States, build a successful company, and sell it in order to feel safe enough to risk a rejection that otherwise could have mortal consequences. I had to run myself ragged personifying ambition to distract myself from the fact that who I projected to the world was in deep misalignment with how I was most comfortable.

I had to break under the pressure of keeping such a large amount of myself in shadow, distancing myself from those I loved. I had to get tired of covering my self-exploration in shame, darkness, and secrecy. And since I began the process of integrating, I have carried a persistent inquiry: "Why was this so hard?" I believe our reunion can help us bring compassion to ourselves as we explore the answers.

We all have queer ancestors. All of us. What did it cost them to hide? Who didn't survive? For those who accepted themselves and their desires, how did they create space for themselves? I know it's impossible to answer these questions. The answers aren't the kind of thing you put in most family histories. So answering these questions is not my goal. Honoring my ancestors, and myself, is. As we ponder the ways that our ancestors have been Othered, have been allied with whiteness or other oppressive systems, we explore the interior and exterior world that they passed down to us. It's up to us to integrate into those worlds or continue to dissociate, disown, and fracture ourselves. The direction we choose has implications for the heart of our organizations, communities, and society.

The history of my family includes stories dating back to

1734. In a carefully preserved record of the history of the Baumanns, my fourth great-grandfather is quoted as saying, "We Baumanns have been accused of ancestor worship." For him, what is described as "ancestor worship" represented the need to inform future generations of their ancestral Belonging.

I am humbled they wrote so much for me. Pieces of me come alive taking in words my ancestors put to paper 150 years ago. As I read each generation describing their ancestors in their own words, I identify strong character traits given to descendants. I see moments of my own upbringing connected to a thread that stretches hundreds of years and across the Atlantic Ocean. In the words of one family patriarch, this history is a "heritage of inestimable value, and far greater than an abundance of material possessions could ever have been."

Devotion to God was a cornerstone value for the Baumanns. As the Swiss population expanded in the second half of the 1800s, Christianity's role in education and daily life was changing. My ancestors came to the United States in part because public education in Switzerland included religious lessons taught by "unbelieving teachers." How could the Baumann children be God-fearing if their teachers were not?

My ancestors departed Switzerland in 1869 and made their way to Ohio. Within a year they purchased a farm in Henrietta Township. In Henrietta, they based their life around the Methodist Church.

But not surprisingly, that carefully preserved history passed down from one generation to the next has no mention of queer identities or relationships. By the time they immigrated to America, Christian ideals about procreative sex were codified into law to discourage what Christians viewed as immoral and deviant sexual behaviors. Even as time marched on and our understanding of sexuality and gender progressed, non-normative expressions were marginalized through medicalization. In the early twentieth century thinking of homosexuality as an identity began to take hold, along with judgments of that identity being unwell, disordered. The values of my family, modeled after the church, did not welcome the expression of homosexuality or queerness.

My ancestors' homosexuality or queerness would have been repressed and likely included mountains of shame and fear. My queer ancestors no doubt experienced dissociative coping mechanisms ranging from deliberate and conscious management of feelings to completely unconscious manifestations of protection. I know that were I born earlier in my family history, I would not have had the luxury of accepting myself in the way that I do now.

When I look back, it's scary to see that self-hate might have been a more "logical" coping mechanism than self-love for many of my ancestors. In the late 1800s and early 1900s expressing queerness meant throwing out the most accessible forms of love, safety, and Belonging.

In my darkest hours, struggling with my own queer inclinations, I had to accept there is no guarantee of safety. Safety was not promised to my ancestors, and it is not promised to me. The conditions of my life simply made safety more likely if I accept and love myself than if I don't. When I had this realization, I began to understand my ambition, my desire to be so far away physically from my family, and the transformative power of a financial safety net. How can we make self-love and self-acceptance safer? It's an elegant question to help us find agency as humans, as leaders.

As was true for our ancestors, some people in power are

making safety and self-acceptance more at odds with one another. In 2022, eighty-seven years after the Reich Office for Combating Homosexuality and Abortion was established, we have an attorney general in Texas who attempted to compile a list of transgender people. This same AG has instructed the Texas Department of Family and Protective Services to investigate parents of transgender children. The government-sponsored animus has forced many families to relocate to other states out of precaution for not only their kids' mental and physical well-being but their entire families' well-being. And Texas is not alone. This year across America legislation banning gender-affirming care and restricting name changes is on the rise. Statehouses in 2018 introduced nineteen bills. In 2022 that number was 800 percent higher. Florida's "Don't Say Gay Bill" in 2022 is attempting to unname, dismember, and unwelcome the parts of us we have barely been able to liberate.

Taking any step to make self-acceptance safer challenges these actors. A rainbow sticker intended to let a student know they are safe, using language with intention to include more people, the curiosity to inspect a feeling or judgment are just a few examples. In some cases, we are taking steps that our ancestors would have been deeply afraid of. In some cases, we are taking steps we are afraid of.

My own journey of leadership and self-acceptance required the closest in my family to inspect their inherited judgments and our ancestors' passed-down sense of safety. My generation of Baumanns includes a larger number of queer identities every year. We will continue doing the work of welcoming the parts of ourselves our ancestors didn't have the opportunity to love.

In my journal, in my thoughts, and in my leadership the

unclaimed queerness in my family is made whole. The ancestors who struggled silently are invited to speak; the shame they carried is allowed to be set down. In this way, my reunion deepens my resolve and gives me strength. My reunion gives me the ability to call on my ancestors to stand behind me when I need the bravery to speak the unspoken, to name the unnamed, and to love the unloved. I imagine when we heal ourselves, we heal our ancestors. I imagine they are cheering for the expansion of our hearts, as extensions of their own. I imagine they can see what we see, feel what we feel, and grow as we grow.

I AM HOME. I AM WITH. I AM CONNECTED TO(O): CHRYSTAL'S STORY

As I was reading an early draft of *Reunion* and ancestors were heavy on my mind, my fifth grader brought home a family history assignment. It was filled with the kinds of questions that assumed a breezy, lighthearted nostalgia and easy answers. They were the questions I knew would surface some wounds and require deeper conversation with my daughter. We worked through the assignment together.

In that spirit, I write for those who have come up out of dust, risen from ash, bloodstained soil; come up out of anonymity, given new names that were not their own, those without perfect bloodlines and traceable pedigrees. I write as a descendant of enslaved people stolen from our ancestral home, brought across what is called the Middle Passage. I write for the descendants of people murdered in the Holocaust, those whose ancestors knew genocide, for people with unknown stories, separated families, those for whom jagged, uncertain, and broken lines leave question marks, penciled-in theories, and dead branches on our family trees. I'm writing so we can feel our own worthiness despite what we have been told, and in spite of what we will never know. We can still contact the broken Belonging from our pasts to honor and mend those painful stories without being undone by them.

To live in an out-group means that, on some level, your sense of Belonging will be predicated upon the motivation and willingness of the dominant group to be inclusive. Extending hospitality and humanity to the Other is often experienced as a threat to one's own position. The difficult work to undo systemic Othering is most often left to those who have the least power to effect change. Marginalized people are expected to do the heavy lifting of bringing people along with us, depleting ourselves in ways that impact our health, safety, and well-being. We expend inordinate amounts of whatever energy we have left to convince others of our worthiness and our humanity, as though we are the ones responsible for having created the conditions of exclusion in the first place.

Reunion is a call to shift the labor back to those who bear the most power to change it; its hope is to rebalance the responsibility so that we are each doing the work that is ours to do. At the same time, I must also resist the urge to assume that the lessons in this book do not apply to me. It may be safe or even tempting to position myself only as the "other," but that would be a dangerous deflection of my own responsibility. I must examine how I, too, am implicated in upholding systems of Othering. If I fail to interrogate my own actions, I risk working in opposition to the greater good. *Reunion* requires each of us to see ourselves more clearly.

It was impossible for me to read this book without exploring my own relationship to Belonging. It is through my life experiences that I am reminded that Belonging and Othering are not distant or abstract concepts. They are the facts and conditions of my existence, amplified by the Black, queer, female body in which I live. I suppose having marginalized identities has a way of doing that to you, making it easy to start in close, working concentric circles outward until the whole picture comes into frame.

While I don't remember the very first time I felt the sense of not Belonging, I do remember the feeling of it in my body from an early childhood dream. I must have been five or six at the time. In the dream, I was standing on the sidewalk in front of the apartment building where I lived in Portland on Tacoma Street, asking, then pleading, and finally screaming so that I would be heard, seen, and felt by my loved ones who were walking past me and through me with hollow eyes, moving toward someone or something in the distance that was not me. The same visceral feeling I experienced in that dream has come back many times throughout my life when I fell out of Belonging. I can still see my small self crumpled on my knees on the concrete, isolated and alone; it is as imprinted now as any waking childhood memory I've ever had.

Even writing of the dream now, I am struck by just how deep and native the desire to belong is. To call it bone-deep, or cellular, even atomic doesn't quite capture it. As humans, we long to belong, in our families, among friends, in our workplaces, our communities, and so on. And yet, there is that which divides and others us, conscious and unconscious acts and human-built systems that sever us from our deepest yearnings and most basic human needs. Choosing tribalism, exclusion, and separation above connection and care undermines the very things we want so desperately. The dissonance between how we live and what will save us is ever-growing.

Creating systems of Belonging, whether as leaders or as humans, means remembering and re-membering all the daily fractures that threaten our wholeness. Belonging is what happens when we decide and act upon the idea that inclusion is vital to our survival, far more than Othering. Belonging is embodying the refrain of "your story is my story" that is echoed throughout *Reunion*. It is, indeed, medicine for the world.

What gives me hope now is that I continue to hear the desire for systemic Belonging spoken into the world through language, justice movements, art, science, and poetry, through murmurs and shouts in the chorus of our shared stories and experiences. For who among us has not felt Othered? It is through this courageous contact with our own silence, exile, and disavowal that we can emerge from this perilous territory of disconnection.

Our responses to Belonging/Othering can be imperfect. I have witnessed and even taken part in that phenomenon of undermining one's own sense of Belonging, or the *never enough* that Jerry writes about. In a well-intentioned effort to avoid the pain of being excluded by others first, I have conspired in joining the effort, creating the very exile for myself that I feared in the first place. Allowed to go unchecked, the legacy of systemic Othering can stealthily twist itself around the psyche resulting in a false safety-seeking, and soul-crushing, preemptive isolation. The more we feel ourselves worthy of Belonging, in the truths of our pasts, the more space we create for ourselves and others to belong. It requires us to stay intact enough to believe in our own worthiness and right to

Belonging in this world, even when we feel inadequate to demand the thing that is our birthright.

When I think of Belonging, I believe there is no one who is not worthy of it. What if we all actually believed and acted as though everyone deserved no less than the holy trinity of love, safety, and Belonging that Jerry speaks of? How would that shift the culture of Othering, violence, and separation that is so destructive? I ask myself these questions and find myself going back again and again to the many origins of the word *belong*, one of which has its roots in the old English *langian*, meaning to grieve for, pine, be pained by, yearn for. As I read this translation, I cannot help but find hope in the ease which comes like an out breath that says *I am home. I am with. I am connected to(o).*

THE CHILD OF A KING IS A SLAVE IN ANOTHER KINGDOM: JOY-TENDAI'S STORY

There is a proverb that comes from one of the indigenous languages spoken in the country in which I was born, Zimbabwe. In chiShona, they say, *"mwana wamambo, muranda kumwe"*— *"the child of a king is a slave in another kingdom."*

I did not fully appreciate the wisdom found in that proverb until as an African woman, now identified as Black, I found myself in a distant country, far from my people, where I have been told many times, and in different ways, that I did not belong. The country I now call home, Ireland, still embraces the complexities of systemic global Othering. I am now part of a society that the "gift" of acceptance and some semblance of Belonging comes from the attachment of colonial labels on my identity and humanity.

While writing this essay, it dawned on me that by choosing to migrate, I became an "other." I would now be viewed through a stereotypical, prejudiced, and even hate-filled lens. I became a "slave in another kingdom."

Speaking honestly, it was the reemergence of the Black Lives Matter movement after the killings of George Floyd, Breonna Taylor, and Ahmaud Arbery—when the American systems of injustice and brutality against Black people were beamed across the world—that I embarked on a journey to reconnect with my roots.

In my new home country, I have been called a "settled foreigner" and "a blow in" by those who choose a polite form of Othering. My children and I have faced overt racism that is rooted in centuries of systemic Othering. The continued use of segregation, apartheid to disenfranchise, target, humiliate, and kill ethnic minoritized bodies sadly means that truly Belonging is unattainable if acceptance and who belongs is defined by the dominant ethnicity. I have learned from my own journey that Belonging is found within you; it is in the heart and mind not dictated by others.

Systemic Othering focuses everything on whiteness forgetting that ethnically marginalized people across the globe have their own indigeneity that cannot be encapsulated in terms such as "BAME" (Black Asian and minority ethnic), "POC," "BIPOC," "dark-skinned," or "colored" labels. When I look at these white-centered acronyms, it is important to clarify that the experience of systemic Othering is not monolithic. The American, African, European, and Asian Othering of Black folks like me is geographic and needs contextual understanding.

In the UK, for example, until recently, BAME was the

socially acceptable term used in policy and academia. It boxed all Black and brown people together on the theory that they all suffered similar systemic injustices. This is quite the contrary, as the Asian community, out of those labeled as POC, hold political, economic power in the UK. Although boxed together with other marginalized ethnic minorities, the Asian community have power, privilege, and proximity to whiteness to perpetuate racial injustices against Black people, as witnessed by the Windrush Scandal, where former UK Home Office Secretary Priti Patel, herself a daughter of South Asian parents who fled Uganda and sought refugee status in the UK, could oversee and wrongly detain, deny legal rights to, threaten deportation of, and wrongly deport at least eighty-three people of Caribbean descent who had lived all their lives, worked, had families, and considered themselves British.

Like the "divide and conquer" mechanism used by colonial powers to subjugate, I have found that it is still used widely as a weapon to maintain a hierarchy of power held by white supremacy. I reflect on this quite a lot as a parent of two Black Europeans. Will a time come when, fueled by the rising right-wing influence in Europe, I and my children will be told to pack our belongings and leave? After twenty years living in Europe, I can say that citizenship does not guarantee acceptance. Nor does it bring you any closer to truly Belonging.

In a world hell-bent on Othering, anti-Blackness and the breaking down and destroying of individuals has been normalized. It has created a generational stream of internalized self-hatred and unrooted people.

As I said before, systemic Othering is specific to geography and context, and as I strongly refuse and will continue to stand against my labeling with white-centered acronyms, I have now come to understand the acceptance by some Black and Indigenous people in the United States of these terms. There is a history, geography, and context to my Black and brown American friends naturally referring to themselves as persons of color (POC) and Black Indigenous people of color (BIPOC). On the other end of the conversation, I always face an internal war with my ancestors who scream at me, urging me never to accept being bound by the chains of white-centered labeling of my identity.

Adjusting to this seismic identity shift can take a toll on the mental and physical health of those who face exclusion. Finding a therapist who understands the nuances of the impacts of not Belonging in your own society can be very difficult. This is because the effects of racial oppression, in my experience, is not only to dehumanize but also to place barriers that stop individuals from finding their power and identity, which helps maintain the cycle of oppression.

Racism comes from a place of chosen ignorance. Recently, at a conference, someone walked up to me and greeted me by someone's else name, someone who I later found out was also Black. I told them I wasn't that person and asked why they would assume I was that person. Their answer was "YOU all look the same." Making other people feel like they do not belong comes not only through building a massive wall across the border or creating tough visa requirements, but also through actions and words that cut deeply to the core of one's sense of self. I have been in white spaces all my life, and I have never mistaken one white person with the next, and I know fellow African or Black people wouldn't either.

The thing is . . . I was born and raised on the African

continent. My ancestors, who faced and fought against brutal racial segregation, also learned the ways of the white colonizers they needed to survive. But they never threw away their customs, language, songs, and traditions. Through apartheid, British colonial rule, they suffered, were brutalized, and were even killed, but it was done with their bodies and minds rooted on the red alluvial soil and in the shade of the acacia trees. These are the cultural values, identity, and history they passed on to me as a child, which, after many years and across many seas, have become my light, shield, and sword.

I am from a tribe of warriors. My totem, *Masibanda* (Lioness), signifies that inside flows the blood of people who fought and triumphed over lions. I stand in their strength and power. I do not have to justify my existence or Belonging to anyone. I can define myself outside the confines of systemic Othering.

I am not a person of color, colored, or any of the other terms that have been created to minimize my existence. I will not be viewed through a lens that aims to Other me. I have and will every time remind myself to emancipate myself from the bondage of systemic labeling when the world casts doubt in my mind.

This message is for my children, and for those who are continually told: *YOU DO NOT BELONG*. We all *belong*, no matter what part of the world we are from or what society we find ourselves living in.

This book tells my story. And my story is a mirror. It is one of loss, separation, seeking acceptance, Belonging, and the great reunion. When I first met Jerry in 2019 at a book reading, little did I know that our ancestors had preordained the meeting. From stranger to mentor and, now, brother, Jerry has taught me that, despite our different paths, we can finally be reunited with those whose stories are our own.

WHAT IS YOUR STORY OF LONGING TO BELONG?

Reuniting with the *stories* of others is part of the journey to that grand reunion where there is no separation and no end to paradise. And, as with every workshop, all who participate have their own stories to share.

To help you find your own story, consider journaling in response to three broad questions. As Parker Palmer wrote in the foreword, the essential first step in this work is to answer Who am I? To get started, journal in response to prompts such as these:

1. How do I identify?
2. Who and what that might relate to that identity have I not seen?
3. How did it benefit me or my family, including my ancestors, not to see or recognize such things?
4. What stories of my family of origin have we chosen to remember and what have we chosen to forget?

The second question Parker notes is broader: *Whose* am I? Journaling prompts that might help you understand this include the following:

1. To whom did my parents belong?
2. What tells me that I belong to my family?
3. What does it feel like to know that I belong?

4. How might I remember the stars and the feel of the wind of the place of my ancestors?

5. Whom among my ancestors might have been left behind or forgotten?

Lastly, consider the question, What is your unique work to do? What is your work that may not be finished but may also not be neglected? To help you find your answer, journal in response to prompts such as these:

1. How have I been complicit in and benefited from systemic Othering?

2. What would I have to give up that I love, that might make me feel safe and that I belong so that others might feel the same way?

3. How might I create systems of Belonging for others?

4. What is my work to lift knees and feet from the necks of others?

5. Whose stories should I be listening to? Whose stories are, after all, my stories as well?

You're welcome to share your stories and responses to the prompts with me at reunion.reboot.io. There you'll find additional material and resources that may support you in your longing to belong.

Finding Kinship

When I began this work, I struggled to understand not merely my responsibility in supporting a community built on systemic Belonging, but my role in bringing such a world into being. Quickly I came to see that my work was to explore my own relationship with my identity as a white, straight, cisgender man, so that I might better listen to those who identify differently. To paraphrase James Baldwin, I had to know from whence I came so that I might contribute meaningfully to others' inclusion, their felt sense of love, safety, and, most importantly, Belonging.

My work, therefore, was to write this book.

What I hadn't realized, though, was how much doing this work would change me. What I hadn't anticipated was that the real work before me, in fact, was for *me* to change. Thankfully, I did change.

For example, in the waning days of writing *Reunion*, I wandered through the halls of the National Portrait Gallery in Washington, DC. I'd gathered with some friends for a weekend to discuss our own stories of Belonging, and we'd decided to walk the gallery for inspiration. We wandered into an exhibit called *Kinship* that featured the works of artists who used portraiture to tell stories of families, of kinship, and, I'd real-ized, of Belonging.

Standing before each work, I found myself feeling the power of kinship. I thought once more of walking through the churchyard where my grandmother rested. I thought of the bones of my ancestors who lay beside her and of how I claimed them as kin.

Prior to writing *Reunion*, I more than likely would have seen the loveliness of those photos and failed to feel the long-ing to belong implicit in each of them.

Before portraits of remarkable people doing the unre-markable work of simply trying to belong to one another, I recalled my lost ancestors. In writing *Reunion*, I'd turned ghosts into elders and thereby experienced the power of kin-ship.

Now, I've come to know that kinship is the felt sense of re-union.

Whether it's in a churchyard in Ireland, or the narrow alleys of a tiny Italian commune, or the halls of a museum in the most powerful city in the world, kinship is everywhere. We merely have to claim it. Indeed, once I claimed those who had been dismembered, I found my own Belonging.

The work of finding and claiming kin was not my only challenge, though. My work, as a writer, was to grow beyond what had come before. When I began writing, I was haunted not only by the dismembered ghosts of my ancestors but also by my own past work. Tossing and turning at night, worry-ing if I would meet the expectations of those who followed my work—my "readers," as my editor once called them—I felt the sharp truth of a favorite line from writer John McPhee. "It doesn't matter that something you've done before worked out well," he wrote. "Your last piece is never going to write your next one for you."

Indeed. Now I see also the wisdom in McPhee's statement. Had I relied only on my past work, had I not struggled through the emotions and memories to create something new and beyond what I'd done before, I would have failed to live up to the importance of the work itself.

I may have failed still. My effort might be riddled with errors and mistakes. If so, those are mine alone. I claim them as I claim the dis-membered parts of myself and kinfolk near and far, past and present. But importantly, if I have failed, it won't have been for a lack of trying; it won't have been for an unwillingness to slay myself.

"And where we had thought to find an abomination, we shall find a God," wrote Joseph Campbell. "And where we had thought to slay another, we shall slay ourselves. Where we had thought to travel outwards, we shall come to the center of our own existence. And where we had thought to be alone we shall be with all the world."

May you, too, come to the center of your own existence for, in that place, you shall know that you are not alone and, more, that you belong.

ACKNOWLEDGMENTS

I have discovered that some folks are as fascinated by the process of writing a book as they are by the book's contents. "How do the ideas come to you?" they'll ask, often then declaring that they don't have the discipline or skill to write.

What their questions and statement reveal, though, is a lack of full appreciation for the process itself. Yes, it's true it takes discipline. For more than two and a half years, for example, I spent hours each weekend staring down the blank sheet of paper that is the bane of a writer's life.

But what folks tend to overlook is that even the solitary process of confronting blank sheets of paper depends on others. That is, it takes kinfolk to bring a book into existence.

As I noted in the introduction, it was the challenge by my daughter, Emma, years ago that caused me to look inward and find the center of my own belonging. Emma, this work is for you. I hope I have been the co-conspirator whom you challenged me to be.

When I first sketched out what I'd planned to do with this book, it was my son Michael who said, "Wow, Dad. That's audacious." Michael, I hope I've earned that look in your eyes when, on the Jersey shore that summer, I shared my plans. This work is for you as well.

There are few things as glorious as the pride one feels in one's children. The only thing that tops that feeling is when you feel their pride in you. Sam, your statement of pride in me that summer in Wales as I bravely read from the far-from-completed manuscript compelled me, energized me, and helped me keep going. I hope to forever be the ancestor you deserve. This work is for you, too.

To my brothers and sisters—Vito, Mary, Nicki, Annie, Dom, and John—thank you for allowing me the space to mine the stories of collective experience. Doing so has helped me make sense of my piece of our lives. I know that, like fingers on a hand, our stories are individually unique and yet bound to one another.

And to Mary and Vito . . . thank you for leading the way in discovering who Dad really belonged to. I would not have made it to Moycarkey were it not for your brave discoveries. And to Nicki . . . thank you for the story of the shawl.

To my nieces, nephews, grandnieces, and grandnephews, may we be the ancestor elders who ensure that you always feel loved and safe, and that you belong.

To Mom and Dad, thank you for my life. I see you now more clearly than ever and, in doing so, love you more deeply than I ever thought possible.

To my grandparents (both named and those unknown) and other ancestors . . . I feel your hands on my back. May I be the descendant worthy of your sacrifices.

Each of us, if we're lucky enough, are blessed by wise elders who tell us when we've gone astray and light the path before us. A very few of us lucky ones are fortunate enough to have elders in our lives with whom we feel a kinship forged in both the heart and mind. Dear Parker Palmer, this work would simply not exist had it not been for your steady kindness, guidance, and loving instruction in the ways we dismember ourselves. Indeed, it's tough to say whether I'd be the man I am today had we not encountered each other, found each other, those many years ago. My brother, this work was done, in part, to honor you.

Dear Sharon, my teacher, you, too, guided my heart and my hand, especially through the thicket of the wages we pay for the violence we inflict on ourselves. I am grateful for your heart, your kindness, and your wisdom.

Jerry Ruhl . . . your wisdom and kindness, too, kept me steady when I struggled with the excavated feelings that came with the recovered memories. Bless you and your work.

To my co-conspirators, Joy-Tendai, Virginia, and Chrystal . . . your stories of belonging propelled and inspired me even as you educated me. Thank you. (And special thanks to JT for giving me the gift of knowing that your story is my story.)

Other co-conspirators in the provoking of systemic belonging include Philippe Celestin and Marshall Pollard, my brothers-in-arms in the great undertaking that is our work to do, even if we may never see it come to pass. Thank you for believing in me.

And to our fellow warriors—Ashanti Branch, Mostafa Wafa, Guarav Manchanda, Carl Desir, and Shawn Dove—for months in our gatherings you each showed the possibility of true and healthy masculinity. You are each an elder, worthy of the word.

To my friend Brad Feld . . . our moments together staring off into the gaping maw of the world and its challenges may be infrequent, but, as a result, each moment is precious. I treasure you.

To Regina Smith and Konda Mason . . . both of you, in your own ways, provoked me to go deeper, to see the relationships between power and identity. From the bottom of my heart, thank you.

To my clients . . . you honor me each and every day by allowing me the privilege of holding your stories. May you always know that you belong.

To my colleagues at Reboot—especially Dan, Jim, Andy, Zane, and Margaret—it is an honor to stand as broken-open-hearted warriors and do this work together. Thanks, too, for allowing my weekly check-in to always begin with "Well, this week I think I made good progress on the book . . ."

Every writer stands on the shoulders of others. This is how we learn. This is how we grow. I am indebted to Ani Pema Chödrön, bell hooks, Lisa Sharon Harper, Rhonda Magee, and Annahid Dashtgard and a host of others, each of whom has done precious and important work in laying the pathways to belonging. Thank you for your work; the world is better because of it.

Thank you, too, Seth Godin, for your mentorship as well as your friendship.

Every writer dreams of finding folks who believe in them. Indeed, without such folks, books wouldn't rise beyond scribbles on blank pages. I am fortunate to have two such folks in my life, each of whom, in different ways, help this project come into fruition. Hollis Heimbouch is the editor with whom every writer should be fortunate enough to work. Even when hangry, her edits make one's prose sing. More importantly, though, she kept me honest and focused on the task before me. To you, dear Hollis (as well as all your colleagues at Harper-Collins), thank you. Thank you not only for believing in me but thank you for your fierce regard for the art of publishing. You prove every day that words matter.

The other believer is my agent, Jim Levine. Jim, unfailingly, and at precisely the right moments, and in precisely the right ways, you kept me grounded and sane. Thank you.

Thank you, Susan Tasaki, for diligently chasing down the permissions needed to give credit where credit is due.

This work would not exist were it not for my partner in life, my better half, my ultimate co-conspirator in bringing love, safety, and belonging to the world, Ali Schultz. Thanks for being my person. Let's stop the world and melt with each other.

Finally, this work was written in part in the shade of a 150-plus-year-old cottonwood. The seeds of this tree took root when the soil was part of the land of the indigenous inono'eino' biito'owu' (Arapaho) and Núu-agha-tʉvʉ-pu̱ (Ute) peoples. Their lands were taken by the United States in treaties that reinforced the unequal power relationship and a dispossession. I acknowledge my complicity in, and benefiting from, this disinheriting and dispossession.

JERRY COLONNA is the CEO and co-founder of the executive coaching firm Reboot.io. A highly sought-after coach and speaker, he is also the author of *Reboot: Leadership and the Art of Growing Up*. For more than twenty years, he has used his experiences as a CEO, investor, journalist, college professor, and, lastly, coach to help people lead with humanity, resilience, and equanimity. He is astounded by the fact that he lives on a farm outside of Boulder, near the foothills of the Rockies and far from the streets of Brooklyn, where he was born and raised. He is the father of three amazing humans, each of whom cares deeply about the love, safety, and belonging of others.